W9-AUM-872

Books by Joan Elma Rahn

Keeping Warm, Keeping Cool

Joan Elma Rahn

KEEPING WARM, KEEPING COOL

WITH ILLUSTRATIONS BY THE AUTHOR

Atheneum   *1983*   *New York*

LIBRARY OF CONGRESS CATALOGING IN PUBLICATION DATA

Rahn, John Elma
Keeping warm, keeping cool.

Bibliography
Includes index
SUMMARY: Describes how living things, especially
animals and human beings, adapt to environmental
temperature changes, in order to conserve heat
in cold weather and lose it in hot weather.
1. Body temperature—Regulation—Juvenile
literature. [1. Body temperature. 2. Temperature]
I. Title.
QP135.R27 1983 591.19'16 83-2620
ISBN 0-689-30995-3

Published simultaneously in Canada by
McClelland & Stewart, Ltd.
Composition by American Book-Stratford Graphics,
Brattleboro, Vermont
Printed and bound
by Fairfield Graphics, Fairfield, Pennsylvania
Designed by Mary Ahern
First Edition

Contents

To Begin

About Body Temperature

What is your body temperature? The answer for nearly everyone is somewhere between 36° and 37°C (96.8° and 98.6°F). A healthy human being has a high temperature that is very close to 37°C during the afternoon and a low temperature near 36°C during nighttime sleep. That is the daily variation—only 1 degree on the Celsius scale (1.8 degrees on the Fahrenheit scale)—of our normal body temperature. A few persons have normal body temperatures slightly higher or slightly lower than this, but usually by less than 1 Celsius degree. A departure of 2 or 3 degrees from the normal temperature usually means that something is wrong, although a rapidly exercising person will have a temporary rise in body temperature that is a normal response to intense activity.

The animal kingdom can be divided into two main groups on the basis of whether or not an animal has full control over its body temperature and keeps at a fairly constant level. However, there is some disagreement about the best terms to be used to describe the group that does and the group that doesn't, because for all the terms used there are some exceptions.

Mammals and birds automatically regulate their internal temperatures with such precision that they rarely vary more than 1 or 2 Celsius degrees regardless of the ordinary temperature variations in their natural environment. Mammals and birds have been described as "warm-blooded" because the temperature of their blood is usually warmer than that of their environment. Nearly all mammals have normal body temperatures between 34° and 40°C (93.2° and 104°F), and nearly all birds have normal body temperatures between 38° and 42°C (100.4° and 107.6°F). Compared with the extremes of temperature that have been recorded in the natural environment on the earth, this range of body temperatures seems very small. The highest official (in shade) air temperature ever recorded was 57.8°C (136°F) in the Sahara Desert; the lowest was −88.3°C (−126.9°F) in Antarctica. Of course, these are extremes, but a temperature of 50°C (122°F) or so is not uncommon in some deserts, nor are winter temperatures of −50°C (−58°F) in polar regions. In each of these climates there are some animals capable of maintaining their normal body temperatures.

All other animals (reptiles, amphibians, fish, insects, and others) are "cold-blooded"; either they do not control their body temperatures at all or they allow it to vary within wide limits. These animals have been called "cold-blooded" because, with their body temperatures the same as that of their environment, their blood is usually cooler than that of a "warm-blooded" animal under the same circumstances. However, on a very hot day, in direct sunshine, a snake (a "cold-blooded" animal) will have warmer blood than a dog (a "warm-blooded" animal) because under these circumstances the snake cannot prevent its blood from heating up, while the dog is automatically cooling his.

The terms most biologists use to describe these two groups of animals are *homeothermic* and *poikilothermic*. In both terms, *-thermic* refers to heat. *Homeo-* means *same,* and *poikilo-* means *variable* or *changing.* Homeothermic animals have constant body temperatures, and poikilothermic animals have changing body temperatures.

Generally, mammals and birds are homeothermic and other animals are poikilothermic, but there are exceptions. In winter, bats, hedgehogs, and ground squirrels enter into a state of hibernation in which their body temperatures drop considerably below the temperatures normal for active animals. A few small birds and mammals experience a temperature drop at night; whippoorwills are small birds that go into a cool, torpid state much like hibernation every night and arouse from it when their bodies warm up in the morning.

eagle

duck

horse

dolphin

HOMEOTHERMIC ORGANISMS

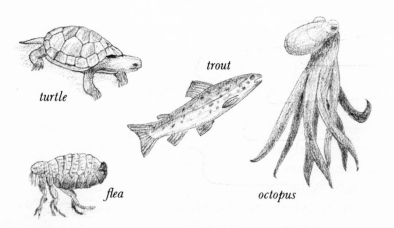

trout

turtle

flea

octopus

POIKILOTHERMIC ORGANISMS

Examples of homeothermic (above) and poikilothermic (below) animals.

Camels are mammals, which are generally homeothermic, but camels do have some poikilothermic tendencies. When a camel has not drunk water for a long time (which can be seen by the shrunken appearance of the body), it cannot maintain a constant body temperature. When a camel has drunk all the water it wants (like the plump camel on the right), it maintains a constant body temperature.

Camels are well known for their ability to survive for a week or more without water in the heat of the desert. When they are well watered, individual camels maintain their body temperatures within a range of 2 degrees—about 36° to 38°C. However, if it has been a long time since they drank, they become slightly poikilothermic, and their body temperatures may drop to 34.2°C (93.6°F) in the cool of the night and may rise to 40.7°C (105.3°F) during the day. We would suffer from such extreme body temperatures, but they seem to do no harm to camels. Once camels drink their fill again, they become homeothermic until they are deprived of water once more.

Individual insects generally are poikilothermic, but some insects that live in colonies—honeybees and termites, for example—can regulate the colony temperature quite precisely. Even some moderately large individual insects, such as bumblebees, can warm up their flight muscles by shivering them while the early morning air is still cool.

Another set of terms used to describe the two main groups of animals are *endothermic* and *ectothermic*. *Endo-* means *inside,* and *ecto-* means *outside.* These terms, as used here, are based on the main sources of heat that warm the animals. Mammals and birds are endothermic because most of the heat that warms them comes from chemical reactions occurring within the body. Other animals are generally ectothermic: most of the heat that warms their bodies comes from the environment, especially from sunshine. However, a bumblebee, an ectothermic animal, produces a significant amount of heat within its muscles when it shivers. A cat, an endothermic animal, basking in sunshine receives a great deal of heat from its environment.

The terms in each of the two columns on the next page refer generally to the same organisms; however, we should mention again that there are exceptions to all of them.

Both ways of life have their advantages and disadvantages. Homeothermic animals can be active over a wide range of environmental tempera-

Mammals and birds	All other animals (*reptiles, amphibians, fish, insects, and others*)
"Warm-blooded"	"Cold-blooded"
Homeothermic (constant temperature)	Poikilothermic (variable temperature)
Endothermic (warmed by inner heat)	Ectothermic (warmed by external heat)

tures. They can flee immediately at any time if they become aware of danger. However, maintaining a constant body temperature requires a great deal of energy, and this comes from food. Homeothermic animals must find and eat more food than poikilothermic animals of the same size.

Poikilothermic animals cannot move rapidly if their bodies are very cool; and if they are very hot, running would only heat them more, perhaps to the point of death. Poikilothermic animals are better off resting and hiding during the coldest and hottest parts of the day, but then they cannot be seeking food or eating at these times. However, because they do not spend a great deal of energy in maintaining body temperatures, they do not need as much food as homeothermic animals of the same size.

Whatever the type of organism, its body temperature represents a balance between the heat produced by chemical reactions within the organism, the heat absorbed by the organism from its environment, and the heat lost by the organism to its environment:

$$\begin{array}{c} \text{heat produced} \\ + \\ \text{heat absorbed} \end{array} = \text{heat lost}$$

As long as the two sides of the equation are equal, the body temperature remains constant. If the left side exceeds the right side, the equation no longer balances, and body temperature rises. If the right side exceeds the left side, body temperature drops. Eventually, the equation may be in balance again but perhaps at a higher or lower temperature.

In homeothermic animals, even a slight change in one side of the equation is balanced almost immediately by a change in the other side. If, for instance, a homeothermic animal increases its activity and so the body produces more heat, almost immediately the body will begin heat-losing processes. Then either the body temperature does not rise, or it does so only slightly and returns to normal when the strenuous activity ceases. If a homeothermic animal begins to lose heat faster than it is producing and absorbing it, the body immediately begins to produce and/or absorb more heat, and there is hardly a variation in temperature.

In completely poikilothermic animals, body

temperature rises and falls as the environmental temperature rises and falls. The equation above can be in balance at any temperature compatible with life. Many poikilothermic animals, however, can regulate heat-producing, heat-absorbing, and heat-losing processes to some extent and prevent their body temperatures from rising or falling to lethal levels.

The processes that keep body temperatures of animals at safe levels are the subject of most of the rest of this book. The book is divided into three parts. The first, and shortest, part deals with what heat and cold are and how heat is transmitted from one body to another. The second part deals with the ways animals adapt to temperature extremes. This includes the ways their bodies respond automatically or nearly automatically to heat and cold. It also includes some instinctive activities such as nest building and migration. The third part of the book discusses the ways human beings use clothing and buildings to help maintain a comfortable artificial environment around them.

Part I

Heat & Cold

1 · What Are Heat and Cold?

Heat is something, but it is not a "thing"; that is, it is not a substance like stone or water or air. Heat is a form of energy. As such it has no shape, no weight, no color, and no odor.

Heat exists in either of two forms: as *molecular motion* or as *radiation*. All objects consist of submicroscopic particles called atoms, and in nearly all substances atoms are grouped into somewhat larger submicroscopic particles called *molecules*. These molecules (as well as single atoms) are constantly in motion, even though this is not visible to us. Even in objects that appear to us to be perfectly still these particles are in motion. The faster they move, the warmer the object is. One form of heat, then, is the energy of the motion of the molecules and atoms that make up all the substances in the universe: rocks, wood, snow, air, plants, animals, you, me, and any other physical objects that you can think of. In solid objects, the molecules do not move far. You might picture them each vibrating

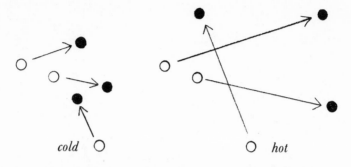

In a cold substance the molecules move slowly. If the same substance is hot they move faster and therefore farther in the same period of time.

about in their "own" space. In liquids, molecules move freely among each other, and in gases they move even more freely.

Heat also exists in the form of radiation called *infrared radiation.* Two other forms of radiation that we will be concerned with in this book are *visible light* and *ultraviolet radiation.* Visible light includes the rainbow colors: violet, blue, green, yellow, orange, and red. Neither infrared nor ultraviolet radiations are visible to the human eye. Radiation can exist independent of physical objects; that is, it can exist in a vacuum, where there are no atoms or molecules.

Radiations move through space as if they were waves, something like the waves that result when you drop a stone into water—but the waves are not visible to the eye. The wavelengths of infrared radiation are longer than those of red light, and the wavelengths of ultraviolet radiation are shorter than those of violet light. There are radiations of still longer and shorter wavelengths, but they do not concern us here.

The energy of molecular motion and the energy of infrared radiation are interchangeable. When infrared radiation reaches some physical material that absorbs it, the molecules in that material move faster and the material becomes hotter. On the other hand, as a hot object cools and its molecules move more slowly, the energy that its molecules lose is radiated away as infrared radiation.

The wavelengths (in nanometers) of visible light and its relation to ultraviolet and infrared radiations.

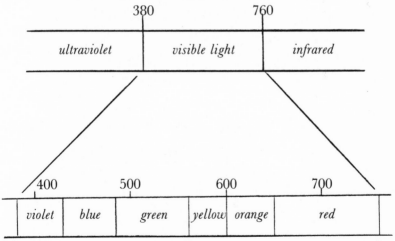

Heat can be transferred from one place to another or from one object to another, and it moves in either of three ways: *conduction, convection,* and *radiation.*

Conduction

The transfer of heat by conduction depends on the motion of molecules; therefore conduction occurs only in some physical substance. When one end of an object, a metal rod, for instance, is heated in a fire, the molecules in that end of the rod begin to vibrate more rapidly. They are now more likely to bump into adjacent, cooler molecules. When the hotter, faster-moving molecules hit cooler, slower molecules, some of their energy is transferred to them, and the formerly cooler molecules become hotter and faster. These molecules are then likely

Conduction of heat occurs when the hotter, faster-moving molecules bump into slower, cooler molecules and transfer some of their heat to them.

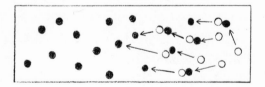

to hit the adjacent molecules a little farther along the rod and transfer their energy to them. In this way heat is conducted down the metal rod. As long as one end of the rod remains heated in the fire and the other end is in a cooler environment, heat will be transferred by conduction from the hotter to the cooler end.

In conduction, the substance that conducts heat does not have to move. The heat is conducted through the metal because the vibrating molecules transfer the heat energy from one to another.

Different substances conduct heat at different rates. Most metals are good conductors of heat: that is, they conduct it rapidly. Almost everyone who has done more than a little cooking has discovered this, because a metal spoon left in a pot on the stove for a few minutes will become too hot to handle. In fact, if you hold a piece of metal in your bare hands and put the far end into the flame, almost instantly the metal will become too hot to hold. In fact, if you don't drop it immediately, you could get a nasty burn.

There is another, safer—though less dramatic—way to demonstrate the rapid conduction of heat by metals. Choose a piece of metal that has been lying for a while in the shade in an ordinary room where the temperature is about 20°C (68°F). A few degrees warmer or cooler will not matter. If the metal object has been there for a while, you will know that it is the same temperature as the room and therefore cooler than your body, which is at 37°C (98.6°F). If you touch most nonmetallic objects in the room (cloth, paper, or the carpet, for instance) they will not feel particularly cool. If you touch the metal object lightly with your fingertip, for a very short period of time—a second or so—it may feel about as warm as the other objects, but then it will suddenly feel cool. This is because the metal is conducting heat away from your fingertip, and this cools your fingertip.

Water is not as good a conductor of heat as metals, but it does conduct heat rapidly enough to have a definite chilling effect on the warmer body placed in it. Furthermore, it takes a great deal more heat to warm a given quantity of water than it does to warm an equal quantity of most other substances. In other words, water can absorb a great deal of heat and still not warm up very much.

Because living things are generally quite small compared to ponds, lakes, streams, or oceans, organisms that live in or venture into them are in a substance that has an almost endless capacity for taking heat from them. This is why people dressed in ordinary bathing suits can survive only a few minutes in ice-cold water, but in dry bathing suits they can remain alive considerably longer in still air at the same temperature. This is also the reason people go swimming to cool off in the summer; as long as the water temperature is somewhat lower than their body temperature, water will conduct heat away from their bodies.

Some substances are very poor—or slow—conductors of heat. Air conducts heat at a rate of only 1/25 that of water. Air is such a poor conductor of heat that we use it in most forms of insulation. Insulation, which we will consider again in later chapters, is something that is used to prevent the transfer of heat to or from an object.

A vacuum is the poorest conductor of heat because conduction depends on the bumping of molecules into each other, and a true vacuum contains nothing, there are no molecules to bump into each other. In actual practice, it is difficult to create a true vacuum, but even the partial vacuum that exists between the walls of a thermos bottle provides good insulation. Outer space, between the planets and the stars, contains so few substances that it is very nearly a true vacuum. Virtually no heat can travel from one celestial body to another by conduction.

The rate at which heat is conducted also depends in part on the difference in temperature of the object it is leaving and the object it is traveling toward. The greater the difference in temperature, the faster heat moves. Suppose you have a metal rod with one end heated to 100°C (212°F) and the other end chilled to 0°C (32°F), and suppose you

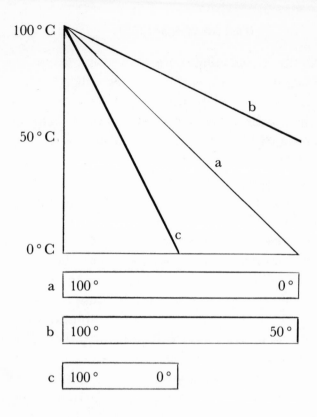

a	100°		0°
b	100°		50°
c	100°	0°	

*Temperature gradients. The
temperature gradient of bar a is steeper
than that of bar b, but the temperature
gradient of bar c is steepest of all.*

have another metal rod of the same size and shape
with the ends at 100°C and at 50°C (122°F). In
both cases heat will move from the hotter end to
the cooler end, but it will move faster in the first

bar, because the difference in temperature is greater.

The rate at which heat is conducted also depends on the distance it travels. If a short metal rod and a long metal rod each have one end heated to 100°C and the other end chilled to 0°C heat will be conducted faster in the short rod than in the long one.

Where there is a difference in temperature we speak of *temperature gradients.* A sharp drop in temperature is a steep temperature gradient.

Convection

Convection, like conduction, occurs only in physical substances; it does not occur in a vacuum. Convection is a type of transfer of heat that depends on the movement of heated gases or liquids. When substances are heated, they expand, and the molecules in them move a little farther apart. This

*When a substance is heated it expands
and the molecules in it are farther apart.*

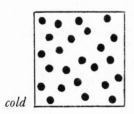 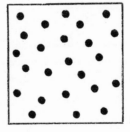

cold   hot

means that in a given volume there is less material. Another way of saying this is that when a substance is heated it becomes lighter or less dense. When a gas becomes less dense than the gas around it, it begins to rise; when it becomes more dense than the surrounding gas, it sinks. Therefore hot (less dense) air rises, and cold (more dense) air sinks. As the hot air rises, it carries the heat with it. Such a current of air is called a *convection current*.

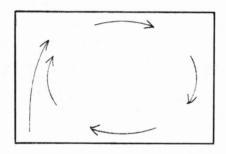

*When air (or water) is heated,
the lighter, hotter air (or water)
rises in a convection current.
Inside a closed container the
current circles around as the cooler
air (or water) descends.*

The greater the difference in temperature of the rising and falling air (or water), the faster will the convection currents rise.

Convection currents also occur in liquids. If a pot of water is heated from below, the hot water rises, and the cooler water sinks.* As the hot water rises, it carries the heat with it.

Radiation

The transport of heat in the form of infrared radiation does not require the presence of physical matter. Infrared radiation does move through air, but it also moves through a vacuum. The heat of the sun comes to us in the form of infrared radiation that travels across 93 million miles of empty space.

This radiation does not warm anything until some physical matter absorbs it. As it travels through the cold vacuum of space virtually none of it is lost. Only a little infrared radiation is absorbed by the earth's atmosphere. The rest is absorbed by

---

* There is an exception to this statement. Water is unusual in being most dense at 4°C (38°F). When water becomes colder than this, it becomes less dense. Therefore, between 4°C and 0°C (32°F, the freezing point of water), colder water rises and warmer water sinks. This is why ice forms first at the top of a lake or puddle rather than at the bottom.

the ground, bodies of water, and living things. Once absorbed, infrared radiation causes molecules to vibrate faster and so heats the substance that absorbed it.

Radiation from the sun also includes visible light, which is composed of the rainbow colors. All these colors together appear white. If an object reflects visible light of all wavelengths, that object appears to us to be white. If it reflects only some of these wavelengths and absorbs others, the object appears to be colored. If, for example, it absorbs all wavelengths except those that are in the green range and reflects green, then the object appears to us to be green. The light that the object absorbs—in this example all the rainbow colors but green—causes molecules to vibrate and warms the substance. The more visible light an object absorbs rather than reflects, the more the object is warmed. If an object absorbs all the wavelengths of visible light, it appears black to us. Darkly colored objects, especially black ones, warm up rapidly in sunshine. White and lightly colored objects are poor absorbers of light and therefore warm up slowly in sunshine.

Ultraviolet radiation, which is invisible to our eyes, may, like visible light, be reflected or be absorbed and converted to molecular energy that warms.

Heat Versus Cold

So far we have talked only of heat. What about cold? What is it? In our everyday lives we tend to think of cold as the opposite of heat, but there really is no such thing as cold. What we call cold is really the absence of heat. Actually, there is no place on earth where there is a total absence of heat. Even during the bitterest cold days of winter there is always some heat in the air—there is just a lot less heat than most of us would desire. If you put your hand on a piece of ice, you might say that you feel the cold, but what you really feel is something with less heat in it than your hand has. Heat is being conducted from your hand to the ice, and this is what makes your hand feel cold. There is no "cold" moving from the ice to your hand.

What we call cold, then, is what we perceive to be cold, and what we call hot is what we perceive to be hot. Both judgments depend on how much heat is present. They also depend on how much heat we are accustomed to having in our environment. An Indian who lives in the tropical rain forest of Brazil probably would think of 10° C (50° F) as cold; an Eskimo might find that warm.

There are two main sources of heat that warm living things. One is heat produced by chemical reactions occurring inside an organism. All these chemical reactions within a living being are called *metabolism,* and nearly all of them release heat. The higher the rate of metabolism, the more heat the body produces. Ordinarily the metabolic rate rises when the body is active. This is why we feel warmer after strenuous physical activity than after taking a nap. Our metabolic rates also increase in cold weather; this prevents a drop in body temperature. The other source of heat for living things is the heat they absorb from their environment— by conduction and convection from air, soil, and water; and by radiation from the sun, from fires, and from objects warmer than they are.

There are two corresponding ways of cooling living things: by slowing metabolism (usually by decreasing activity), and by transferring heat from the body to the environment.

The balance at any one moment between the heat produced and gained and the heat lost determines an animal's body temperature.

The rest of this book is devoted to the ways that some animals adapt to the extremes of hot and cold environments by altering the rates of these processes.

Part II

How Animals Keep Warm & Cool

2·Through the Surface

When an animal receives heat from its environment or loses heat to it, that heat must pass through the animal's surface. How fast heat can be exchanged with the environment depends in part on how much surface area the animal has and this is determined by the animal's size and shape. Also affecting the rate of heat exchange are the animal's color and the amount of insulation it has at its surface.

Size and Surface

Suppose we let a very simple geometric figure—a cube—represent an animal. If this cube is 1 inch on each edge, then its volume is 1 cubic inch. Its surface area is 6 square inches, for each face has an area of 1 square inch.

Now imagine that we cut the cube in half.

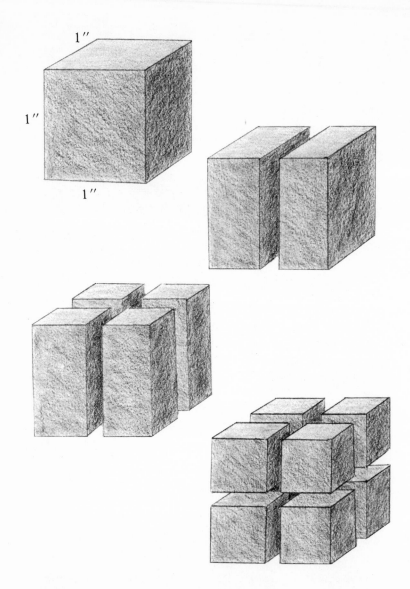

1″

1″

1″

If a cube is cut into smaller and smaller pieces the total amount of surface area increases, but the volume of material remains the same.

Each piece has one new face with a surface area of 1 square inch. In other words, we have added 2 square inches of surface area, but the total volume of material has remained the same.

If we cut these pieces in half at right angles to the first cut, we will add 2 more square inches of surface area. If we cut the resulting pieces once again at right angles to both of these cuts, we will add 2 more square inches of surface area. We will also have made eight small cubes out of the original, larger cube.

The eight small cubes have the same volume as the original large cube (1 cubic inch), but together they have twice as much surface area, because the three cuts added 6 square inches to the original 6 square inches. Each small cube has twice as much surface area in relation to its volume as the original, large cube did.

This means that if these cubes were animals in a cold environment, and if they originally had the same warm body temperature, the small cubes would be losing heat faster than the large cube as long as the small ones were far enough apart that the heat from one did not interfere with the transport of heat away from the others.

On the other hand, if the cubes were in an environment with a higher temperature than their body heat, they would absorb heat through their surfaces, and the small cubes would warm up faster than the large one.

If you were to calculate surface-to-volume relationships for objects of different shapes (spheres or pyramids, for instance) you would find that while the exact numbers vary, this relationship always holds: for any given shape, the smaller the object the more surface area it has per volume, or, conversely, the larger the object the less surface area it has per volume. Therefore, as long as other things are equal, a large object will lose heat more slowly to a cold environment than a small object, and it will gain heat more slowly in a hot environment.

Another thing to notice is that the center of one of the smaller cubes is nearer the surface than is the center of the larger cube. Heat from the center of the small cube has a smaller distance to travel before it reaches the surface. From the center to the surface, the temperature gradient is steeper for a small object than for a large object of the same shape.

For these reasons, because of their small size, microorganisms (living things so small that they can be viewed only through a microscope) and even some small organisms visible to the naked eye cannot control their own temperature. Although they do produce metabolic heat, in an environment cooler than they are, they lose heat rapidly. In an environment hotter than they are, they gain heat rapidly. In other words, their temperature is very nearly the same as that of their environment.

Very large animals, on the other hand, lose heat slowly in a cold environment, and they absorb heat slowly in a hot one. They ordinarily maintain a high body temperature even in a cold environment because they can produce heat as fast as they lose it.

There is a very general rule that for any given group of more or less closely related species, the largest ones live in or near the polar regions, and the smallest ones live at or near the equator, and intermediate ones live in between. Moose, for instance, are the largest animals of the deer family, and they live mostly in Alaska and northern Canada. Their large bulk is part of the reason they can

Moose, white-tailed deer, and mouse deer.

survive the cold winters and probably remain comfortable during most of it. Somewhat smaller deer,
such as the white-tailed deer, live in temperate regions. The tiny mouse deer—not true deer but
closely related—live in the hot, tropical rain forests
of southeastern Asia and the East Indies; these animals are smaller than many dogs.

There are exceptions to this general rule about
size. If the environmental temperature is higher
than the animal's body temperature, then large
size can be an advantage, for a large body warms
up more slowly than a small one. Camels ordinarily live exposed to the sun and hot air all day. In
the treeless desert there is no escape in shade, and
the camel's large size is one reason it survives there.
Small desert animals, such as rodents, heat up rapidly in the sun; these animals retire to shady spots
or burrows during daylight hours and seek food at
night, when the desert air is cool.

Shape and Surface

Let's return to the 1-inch cube, and imagine beside
it an object that measures 2 inches by 2 inches by
¼ inch. Its volume is the same as that of the cube
(1 cubic inch). However, it has a surface area of 10
square inches, which is more than the 6 square
inches of the original 1-inch cube. Obviously, objects of the same volume can have different shapes

*An object with the same volume as a one-inch
cube, but with more surface area.*

and different amounts of total surface. If two objects have the same volume but different shapes,
the one with the more compact shape will have the
least surface area and the one with the least compact shape will have the greater surface area. If one
with little surface area and one with a lot of surface
area were originally at the same temperature, but
were then placed in a cooler environment, the less
compact one would lose heat faster than the more
compact one because it has more surface area
through which it can lose heat. And, of course, the
less compact object would gain heat faster than the
more compact one in a hot environment.

The most compact shape is a sphere. Although
some microorganisms are spherical in shape or
nearly so, most animals have some kinds of projec-
tions from their bodies: ears, legs, tails, wings, for
instance. The longer these parts are relative to the
size of the animal, the more surface area there is
through which there can be heat loss or gain.

Another general rule is that among animals of related species, those near the poles have shorter ears, and those near the equator have longer ears. The arctic fox, for example, has very short, stubby ears from which it loses relatively little heat. The

A fennec (above), a red fox (left), and an arctic fox (right). Notice the difference in the sizes of their ears.

arctic fox lives the year round in cold regions, and, in winter especially, it needs to conserve all the heat it can. In temperate regions, foxes, such as the red foxes, have ears of intermediate length. In North Africa there lives a foxlike animal called the fennec. Like the desert rodents, it hunts by night and retires by day to a burrow where it escapes the extreme heat of the desert day. Viewed from the front, a fennec seems to be half ears. These big ears probably have at least two functions. They catch sound more efficiently than smaller ears, and so they probably improve the fennec's nighttime hunting. At the same time, because of their relatively great surface area in relation to their volume, the ears act as radiators; this cools the fennec.

A good radiator of heat is also a good absorber of heat. If the environment is hotter than the radiator, the radiator becomes an absorber of heat. So animals with big ears must try to find cool places. Another animal whose ears are big radiators is the jackrabbit; but unlike fennecs, jackrabbits are active by day. Jackrabbit ears have very little hair on them, and they are well supplied with blood vessels. If you look at a jackrabbit's ears with the light coming from behind them, the blood vessels will stand out clearly.

In very hot weather, the jackrabbit seeks shade, but it does not have a burrow. Instead it usually lies in a shallow but shady depression and

A jackrabbit's ears can function as radiators of heat if the jackrabbit rests in shade with the ears exposed to the open sky.

keeps its ears in a horizontal position over its back. In this position it receives no radiation directly from the sun, and very little radiation reflected from rocks, trees, or other objects on the surface of the ground. Above, it is exposed only to the clear blue sky, which radiates virtually no heat toward the ground. The jackrabbit's ears, however, radiate heat upward toward the sky. If the jackrabbit has found a good resting place, the ears can lose as much heat by radiation as the entire animal receives by conduction, convection, and radiation from its environment.

Ears are not the only radiators of heat. The long, bare tails of mice, rats, muskrats, and opossums have the same function. Long, slender legs with little or no insulation also radiate heat rapidly. Some birds have bare, slender legs or thin, membranous webs between the toes, or both.

All these large, exposed extremeties help to radiate away excess heat that cannot be lost through the surface of the rest of the animal's body, either because it is too large and bulky or because it is covered by a thick layer of fur or feathers.

The long, bare legs of flamingos and their membranous feet and the long, bare tails of rats are radiators of heat.

Color

The color of an organism influences its temperature, but it should be pointed out here that color has other functions that may be more important to the organism than regulating temperature. Some colors, for instance, allow animals to blend in with their background and so protect them from predators. Other animals, some poisonous ones and those that mimic them, have very bright colors that predators learn to avoid. In still other species, males and females have different coloration, and it is by color that the two sexes recognize each other. However, whatever the color and whatever its other functions might be, the color of an animal does influence its temperature.

If you ever have occasion to pet a friendly black and white dog that has been in bright sunshine for a while, you will notice that the black part of his coat is much warmer than the white part. This is because black is a good absorber of visible light (which is converted into heat once it is absorbed), but white reflects visible light and is a poor absorber of light. We might expect then that animals living in cold climates would have dark coats and animals living in hot climates would have light-colored coats. This is true to some extent. Desert animals, for instance, often have light tan or cream-colored coats, whereas moose and grizzly bears have coats of darker brown.

However, there are some notable exceptions to this. If dark colors are warmer than white, why are polar bears white? Arctic foxes, arctic hares, and ptarmigans are white in the winter and some other color, brown or gray, in the summer. Wouldn't it be better for these animals to have a dark-colored coat in the winter? The answers to these questions have several parts.

For one thing, the white color of these animals blends well with the white color of snow. Therefore, in winter, white is a protective color on arctic hares and ptarmigans, which are not so easily seen by predators. For the same reason, polar bears and

A mother polar bear and two cubs travelling over snow as they might appear in aerial photographs taken with different kinds of film. With ordinary black-and-white film sensitive to visible light (left), the white bears on white snow would be invisible or nearly so. With film sensitive to only infrared radiation (center), both appear black; the cold snow radiates little heat and neither do the bears with their insulating coats and fat. With film sensitive to ultraviolet radiation (right), the bears appear black and the snow white because the bears absorb ultraviolet radiation but the snow reflects it.

arctic foxes in their white coats can approach closer to their prey than they might if they were dark against the white snow.

In addition, it has been discovered that polar bears' coats absorb ultraviolet radiation. Because we cannot see ultraviolet light, the fact that an animal absorbs it or does not absorb it makes no difference in how the animal looks to us. A white animal that absorbs ultraviolet radiation looks the same to us as a white animal that does not. However, once absorbed, ultraviolet radiation is converted to heat. Therefore, despite reflecting visible light, a polar bear can be warmed by the ultraviolet radiation in sunlight. Several other white animals of polar regions—perhaps all of them—absorb ultraviolet radiation.

Furthermore, even though a white coat reflects away a great deal of visible light, some light does penetrate the coat and it usually goes more deeply into it than it would into a black coat. This is because nearly all the visible light is absorbed at the surface of a black coat and converted to heat there. In a white coat, some visible light is reflected from hair to hair or feather to feather and may reach the skin before it is absorbed and converted to heat. In windy weather, the heat at the surface of a black coat is blown away, but the heat accumulating inside a white coat is protected from the wind. Therefore, in sunny, windy weather, a white coat can be warmer than a black coat; but in sunny, calm weather a black coat may be warmer than a white one. The thickness of the coat and how shiny (reflecting light) it is also affect how warm or cool it may be.

For these reasons, animals of the tropics and deserts may remain cool enough to survive in bright sunshine even though they may have black or dark-colored coats.

Insulation

You will remember from Chapter 1 that air is a poor conductor of heat but a good convector of heat. If air is absolutely still, it will conduct heat away from a warm body only very, very slowly. However, as soon as the air near a hot body becomes warmed up, the air becomes lighter than the cooler air around it, and it begins to rise and convects heat away from the body. If air could be kept from moving and from convecting heat away from a hot body, it would be an excellent insulator.

How can air be prevented from moving? Air seems to be something that moves quite freely. One way of keeping it still is by trapping it in many small spaces so that it cannot move from one space to another or can do so only very slowly. Then the air cannot move by convection, and it can function

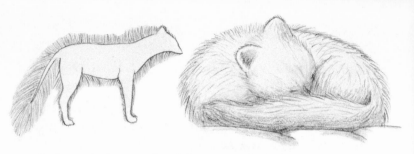

Both arctic foxes and red foxes are relatively small and slim animals, but their fur is so thick that they can sleep comfortably on snow. The hair of the tail is so long that the animals can use it to insulate their faces and paws while sleeping.

only as the poor conductor—or good insulator—that it is.

The fur of mammals and the feathers of birds function as insulators on the surface of the body. Between the hairs or feathers are many spaces, each holding a tiny pocket of still air. The thicker the layer of fur or feathers, the better the insulation is likely to be; for the thicker the insulation, the less steep is the temperature gradient between the living tissues of the animal and the environment.

Generally, animals that live in cold regions have thicker coats of fur than do animals of the same size living in warm regions, and the heavier coats are usually thicker in the winter than the summer. New hairs begin to grow in autumn or early winter, and in spring many of the hairs fall out. Arctic foxes, which are not particularly large animals, and which, therefore, might be expected to lose a great deal of heat in cold weather, remain active during the winters quite far north because they have such luxuriant fur coats. These foxes may even sleep by preference on the snow, rather than retiring into dens. The arctic fox appears to be comfortable at temperatures as low as $-50°$C ($-58°$F)—a fact that tells much about the insulating qualities of its coat. Snow falling on arctic foxes and other animals with thick fur coats in good condition does not melt; this is because almost no heat escapes from the body through the coat.

Generally, the longer the hairs, the better the insulation. Musk-oxen have such long hairs that they may reach nearly to the ground. These animals live on the cold windswept tundras of the northern parts of North America, where there is no shelter from the wind. Yet their large size and long coats make them almost impervious to cold weather.

Very small animals, of course, cannot have such thick coats. A mouse with hair as long as musk-oxen's would be tripping over himself every

Musk-ox.

time he moved. This is another reason why small animals ordinarily cannot survive long when freely exposed to the bitter cold of polar winters.*

Some animals—polar bears and caribou, for instance—have hollow hairs that add even more tiny chambers of air to their coats. This is especially valuable to animals that live in very cold climates, as polar bears and caribou do. In addition, the air spaces among the hairs in a well-kept coat aid an animal in swimming, for they add to the animal's buoyancy. Air in hollow hairs contributes even more buoyancy. Polar bears spend a lot of their time swimming. Although caribou spend most of their lives on land, they do migrate, and when they cross rivers, the air in the hollow hairs must be of considerable help.

Many fur-bearing animals can fluff up their

---

* Some insects, including very small ones, can be active on cold winter days because they contain substances called antifreezes. An antifreeze lowers the temperature at which the water in their bodies freezes. The presence of an antifreeze does not keep them warm; it allows their bodies to become very cold without freezing. How cold they can become without freezing depends on the concentration of the antifreeze in their body fluids. Many of these insects have dark colors that absorb sunlight, and this usually prevents their bodies from reaching temperatures below which the antifreeze is effective.

coats when they are cold. This increases the thickness of the coats and makes them even better insulators. In the skin there is a small muscle called a *pilo-erector muscle* attached to each hair. As long as this muscle remains relaxed, the hair lies flat or at an oblique angle to the skin. When the pilo-erector muscle contracts, it pulls the hair into a more nearly erect position. This is what fluffs up the coat. Pilo-erector muscles contract when the animal begins to become cold.

Human beings also have pilo-erector muscles attached to the hairs all over their bodies. When we

Hair lying "flat" (a) and (b); pilo-erector muscle is relaxed. Hair is erect in (c) and (d); pilo-erector muscle is contracted. The layer of insulation is much thicker in (c) than in (a).

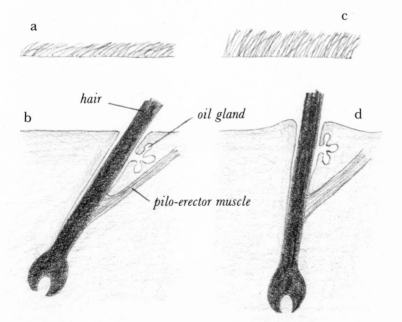

are cold, the muscles pull these hairs up, although the hairs are too fine and too short to provide much warmth. "Goosebumps" are the little bumps caused by the raising of the individual hairs.

Although we usually think of a coat of hairs as retaining heat within the animal during cold weather, in some species it prevents heat from reaching the animals. Camels, who live under hot, dry conditions, have a woolly coat that insulates them from heat. The same is true of species of sheep adapted to desert conditions.

Most feathers that we see when we glance casually at a bird are *contour feathers*. They lie flat, nearly parallel to the surface of the bird, and they overlap each other like the shingles on a roof. Each contour feather has a central *shaft* from which arise branches called *barbs*, and the barbs have smaller branches called *barbules*. The barbules of each barb crisscross the barbules of the adjacent barbs. All this creates many small air spaces that insulate the bird.

An adult bird may have small *down feathers* among the contour feathers, and the first feathers of a chick are down feathers. A down feather has a short shaft with barbs in an irregular, fluffy arrangement. The barbs of down feathers become enmeshed among the barbs of other down feathers. Thus down feathers provide even better insulation than do contour feathers. Female eider ducks—a

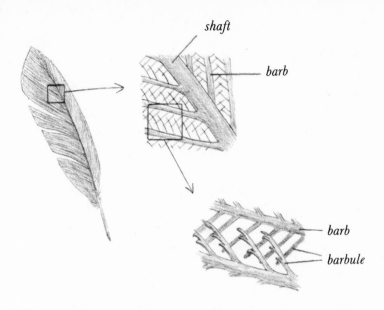

shaft

barb

barb

barbule

A feather showing the many small spaces among the barbs and barbules.

A down feather.

species of duck that lives in northern climates—pull down feathers from their own bodies and incorporate them into their nests. The newly hatched chicks then are protected by a double layer of down insulation—their own and the nest.

Associated with the base of each hair of a mammal is a small gland that secretes oil. Most birds have an oil gland that opens at the base of the back near the tail feathers. When birds and mammals groom themselves with their beaks or paws, they are distributing the oil evenly over their feathers or hairs. As each feather or hair touches its neighbors, the oil forms a seal over the many air pockets below. This is especially important to aquatic mammals and birds, for if water moves into the air spaces, the animals will no longer be insulated. Because water is a better conductor of heat than air is, when water reaches the skin, the animal loses heat quickly. It also loses the buoyancy that the trapped air gave. As long as the hair or feathers remain well-oiled, the layer of insulating air protects the body.

A third type of animal insulation is a thick layer of fat under the skin. This fat, called *blubber,* is present in whales, seals, and other marine mammals, especially those of cold waters. Most of these animals have only a thin covering of short fur that provides little insulation. The skin is cold, often only about 1°C (33.8°F), but the vital parts inside

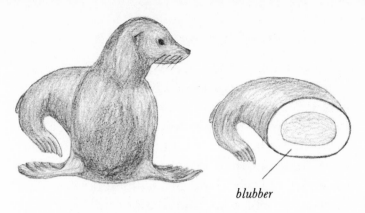

blubber

A seal has a thick layer of blubber under the skin. An adult seal is usually a little more than half blubber.

the blubber are kept warm. Presumably the animal is not uncomfortable with its skin temperature near that of ice.

As a general rule, terrestrial animals of polar regions are insulated by fur or feathers and aquatic animals by blubber. Animals that live both on land and in the sea have both an outer layer of fur or feathers and a layer of blubber below the skin. Usually, however, either one or other provides most of the insulation.

Penguins, which live part of the time in water and part on land or ice floes, have a layer of blubber under their skins, but this seems to function only as a food reserve and not as insulation. Emperor penguins of Antarctica, which live through what are probably the coldest, fiercest winters anywhere on earth, have the thickest, most closely packed coat of feathers of any species of bird. Their skin temperature is almost as high as their interior temperature; this means that the feathers provide the insulation—not the blubber.

A polar bear, on the other hand, has long but rather loose fur that is easily parted by a breeze or penetrated by water during swimming. Although the coat provides some insulation, the polar bear gets most of its protection against cold water and cold air from its fat.

Animals of hot climates do not have a thick

Some varieties of animals store fat in only one part of the body—the tail of fat-tailed sheep and the hump of zebu cattle.

layer of fat under the skin; this would interfere with heat loss. Those hot-climate animals that do store significant quantities of fat usually have it in one relatively small part of the body where it interferes as little as possible with the loss of heat—for example, the humps on the backs of many breeds of cattle from the tropics and long, thick tails of fat-tailed sheep.

A camel's hump, by the way, stores fat, not water. Contrary to popular opinion, a camel does not store water at all. A camel becomes dehydrated when it does not drink for several days. When it does have the opportunity to drink, a camel merely replaces what it has lost.

3 · Behavior: Taking Care of Oneself

Just being the appropriate size, shape, and color and having a layer of insulation is not all there is to maintaining constant temperature. Nearly all animals of sufficient size and strength to have control over at least some of their bodily movements can modify their temperatures to some extent by their behavior.

One of the simplest ways to prevent heating up or cooling down is just to move from a warm place to a cool one or vice versa. This is important for both homeothermic and poikilothermic animals, but especially for the latter. If poikilotherms have a choice of environments in which to spend their time—for example, cool burrows, shade under a bush, or direct sunshine—they will ordinarily select the place that will keep their body temperatures nearly constant. By their choice of environment, poikilotherms can sometimes keep themselves very nearly homeothermic. Of course, such a wide choice of temperatures is not always available in every habitat.

Retiring to Burrows

Animals of hot deserts—especially the smaller animals—sleep in the shade or in burrows by day and come out and hunt by night.

In cold climates animals generally hunt by day and sleep in underground burrows or under the snow at night. Birds usually take shelter in evergreen trees or under low, thick shrubs. Lem-

Desert animals usually retire to shady spots or burrows during the heat of the day.

mings, mice, and other small rodents, which would die if exposed for long to the cold air, survive the entire winter under the snow. During summer and autumn, rodents lay up a supply of food in or near their burrows. They may make temporary tunnels in the snow, but if they have a good supply of food, they do not have to come up into the air until spring.

In addition to providing protection from wind and storms, underground burrows also provide a moderate, more nearly uniform temperature than does the air above ground, whether in a desert or the arctic tundra. This is because the ground itself is an insulator. The soil is made of many small particles, among which are tiny air spaces that insulate the underground burrow from the temperatures above. In fact, except for extremely cold places where the ground is frozen the year around, at a depth of perhaps 2 or 3 meters (about 6.5 to 10 feet)—the exact depth may vary from place to place and with soil conditions—the temperature may not vary more than a degree or two from, let us say, 13°C (55.4°F) all year around. In hot weather or cold, if an animal digs a burrow sufficiently deep, it ought to be able to find a very comfortable place to rest during the day.

In snowy regions, snow makes an added blanket of insulation above the ground, for there are small air spaces between the individual flakes, and

Snowflakes have intricate patterns. As they fall on each other many small air spaces are formed that insulate the ground below from the cold temperatures of the air above.

in addition, most snowflakes are rather finely divided, making even smaller air spaces. A blanket of dry, fluffy snow about .75 meter (about 2.5 feet) deep keeps the soil only 2.5 centimeters (1 inch) below the surface virtually as warm as the soil at greater depths. A rodent with only a shallow burrow in soil covered with a thick layer of snow can spend most of the winter in a comfortable home and never have to experience temperatures below that of the snow itself, and that only when the animal has to make trips to nearby stores of food. This is much better than having to face air temperatures of −40° or −50°C sometimes combined with high winds.

Where the ground freezes, just the snow itself

can be a form of shelter. Although it may seem a cold place for us, a snowbank does protect from winds and is certainly better than the open air. Wolves, sled dogs, and some other animals with thick fur dig temporary shelters in the snow when they have nowhere else to sleep. Because there are so many small air spaces in snow, there is no danger of smothering under just a few feet of ordinary snow, for there is plenty of oxygen to breathe.

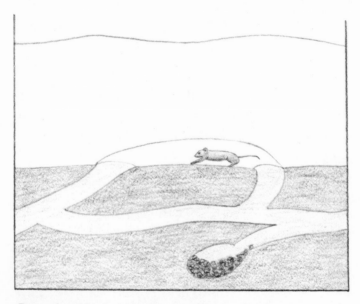

Beneath a blanket of snow small animals like the meadow mouse can remain active throughout the winter if they have stored an adequate supply of food in their burrows.

Occasionally human mountain climbers and other outdoorsmen who find themselves stranded in a snowstorm with no means of lighting a fire save themselves by curling up in the snow. They may spend a miserable night with danger of frostbite, but even that is better than wandering aimlessly in a storm and perhaps freezing to death.

Large animals, such as moose or caribou, which cannot burrow in the snow, take shelter as best they can among trees, where the force of the wind is broken at least somewhat. However, because of their great size, which slows heat loss, they do not have so great a need for shelter as do smaller animals.

Orienting to the Sun

Another very simple way for an animal to exert some control over its body temperature is for it to change its position relative to the sun. Camels, which often can find no shade in the desert, lie down at midday facing the sun; this exposes less surface area to sunlight.

Lizards that live in the desert usually begin their mornings, when the air and ground are still cool, by basking in the sun. During the night their body temperatures usually have fallen, and they cannot move quickly enough to catch prey or to escape predators until their bodies warm sufficiently.

During its early-morning basking, a lizard presents its side to the sun; this way it exposes the greatest possible amount of body surface to light. Later, as the day becomes warmer, the lizard faces the sun; this presents a smaller surface area to the light. The lizard also chooses warmer or cooler ground —whichever is appropriate. When the day becomes still hotter, the lizard seeks shade or a burrow.

The coloration of a basking animal is also important. Some lizards change color with temperature. If their body temperature falls, their skin becomes darker, and they absorb more of the light that strikes them. When body temperature rises, the skin becomes paler and reflects more of the light away. Elephants sometimes spray themselves with dust of a lighter color than they are; this has a temporary cooling effect.

When light strikes a surface at an oblique angle, it warms that surface less than when it strikes it at a right angle, for the same quantity of light spreads out over a larger area at an oblique angle than it does at a right angle. If two surfaces are of different colors, then the amount of light absorbed depends on both the color and the angle at which light strikes that color.

Herring gulls are white and gray. The head, neck, and breast are white; the wings and back are gray. If a herring gull faces the sun, light falls most directly on the white parts. The gray parts receive

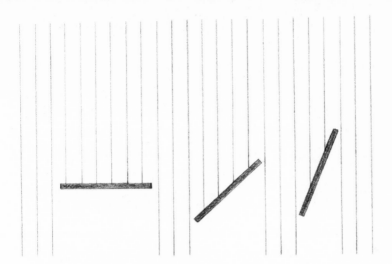

If a flat surface is perpendicular to light rays it receives
more light than if it is oblique to the light rays.

light at an oblique angle or are shaded. Therefore, the white parts reflect most of the light received, and the darker, gray parts receive as little light as the bird can arrange. Herring gulls stand in this position when the day is hot.

On the other hand, if a herring gull stands with its side or back to the sun, then at least some of the gray parts receive light at right angles or nearly so. In this way, the bird is warmed as much as possible by the sun. Herring gulls stand in this position on cold days. It does not matter much at what angle the white parts receive light on cold days, for these reflect most of the light received anyway.

*In warm weather herring gulls face the sun; this way
little light strikes the gray parts. In cold weather herring
gulls face away from the sun or present their sides to it;
then light strikes the gray parts nearly perpendicularly.*

You probably have seen pictures of flocks of
birds or herds of animals in which nearly every individual was facing in the same direction. If the
picture was taken on a sunny day, it is quite possible that they were doing so because the day was
either hot enough or cold enough that they were all
comfortable only in one position relative to the
sun.

Reducing or Increasing Exposed Surface Area

If you have a pet dog or cat, you have probably noticed that the animal sleeps in different positions and that these positions are influenced by the temperature of the environment. In very hot weather, in addition to seeking shade, a dog or cat usually lies on its side and stretches out as much as possible with the head forward, the legs at right angles to the body, and the tail also extending from the body. This exposes a maximum amount of surface area through which the animal loses heat to its environment.

In the winter, the animal seeks sunshine, and if it finds a warm enough patch of sunshine, it may lie in the same position as in the summer, exposing as much surface area as possible to the light, but in this case the animal is absorbing light and keeping warm instead of cool. If the animal cannot find a warm enough spot in the winter, if will lie curled up with its legs tucked close to the body, the head pointing backward, and the tail, with its coat of hairs, brought forward and covering the nose. All this reduces the amount of surface area exposed to the air, and thereby reduces the amount of heat lost. The animal has made itself as nearly spherical as possible. Very large dogs, especially those with thick coats, may not have the habit of curling up except when they are outdoors in cold weather.

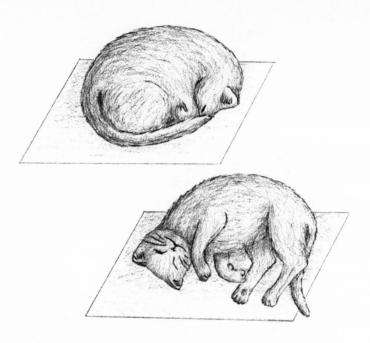

In cold weather a cat curls up and presents as little surface area as possible; the tail hairs insulate the bare nose. In hot weather the cat stretches out and presents as much surface area as possible; the lengths of the legs and tail are all exposed to the air.

Their size and the insulation provided by their coats are enough to keep them comfortable in moderately cold weather.

In hot weather, birds may stand with their wings outspread. This increases the total surface area exposed to air; it also exposes the lower surface of the wing, which has few feathers and, so, less insulation. Birds that are cold fluff their feathers and either sit on their feet or draw one foot up into the coat of feathers. Many of them sleep with the head tucked under one wing. All this makes the overall shape of the body more nearly spherical.

A grass snake exposing as much surface area as possible in hot weather.

Snakes are poikilotherms. With their long, slender shape and the ability to curl up in a series of coils, they can adapt to variations in temperature. Stretched out in the sun on a cool day, a snake exposes a maximum amount of surface area through which it can absorb light. Curled up, with its coils overlapping or touching each other, the same snake reduces its exposed surface area and conserves heat on a cool, overcast day or at night. Some female snakes warm their eggs by curling around them.

Huddling together is another way of reducing the amount of surface area exposed to the environment. Where two animals with the same body temperature touch, there is no temperature gradient, and so they do not gain or lose heat there.

Social animals, which live in herds, packs, or flocks, often come closer together in cold weather.

A female python incubating her eggs.

In very cold weather the entire group may be huddled together in what amounts to one large mass. Young animals that were born the preceding spring or summer and have not yet achieved full size are, because of their smaller size, more likely to lose heat than are the adults. These young ones usually stay somewhere in the middle of the group, where conditions are warmer.

If you have ever seen a sleeping litter of puppies or kittens, you know that they often sleep in a heap, one on top of the other. Again, because they are so small individually, they lose heat faster than their parents do, but the little ones conserve heat by sleeping close together. If their mother is nearby, they snuggle against her.

Ordinarily, we would usually find huddling together on a hot day uncomfortable, because it slows down loss of heat from the body. However,

A litter of puppies keeping warm in cold weather.

In very hot weather camels huddle close to each other because they absorb less heat from another camel than from the air. By facing the sun at the same time, they receive as little sunshine as possible. Their raised heads shade at least part of their long necks.

when the environmental temperature is higher than body temperature, huddling slows down heat gain. Under such conditions, resting camels huddle together. If the air temperature is 45° or 50°C (113° or 122°F), as it may be during the day in some deserts, another camel, whose temperature may be about 40°C (104°F), is more comfortable to the touch than is the air.

Keeping Cool with Water

Barnyard pigs have earned a reputation for being dirty because they often wallow in mud. Yet it is not so much the mud they seek as the water in the mud. On a hot summer day, water feels cool. Most of us find an hour or two in a pool or lake a most delightful way of passing part of a summer afternoon. Because water is a better conductor of heat than air, we lose heat faster in water than in still air. That is why pigs find relief in mud when clean water is not available to them. Elephants, too, enjoy bathing and will spend time splashing in a stream or water hole, and shore birds stand with their feet in water.

There is more to cooling by water than just conduction, however. Water evaporates, and evaporation has an additional cooling effect.

The molecules of water in liquid water—as in all other substances—are in constant motion, and the warmer the molecules, the faster they move. Water evaporates when water molecules break through the surface and into the air. Once liquid water has evaporated, it becomes water vapor in the air.

The molecules at the surface of the water are in a somewhat closer formation than the molecules below. Unless a liquid water molecule below is moving fast enough, it cannot break through this surface. Thus the warmer, faster molecules have a greater probability of breaking through the surface; they are the ones that have the greatest probability of evaporating. Therefore, the warmer the water—heated by whatever means, conduction,

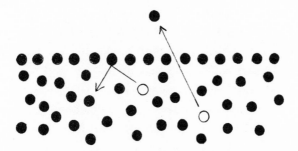

In a body of water, the molecules at the surface are more closely and uniformly arranged than the molecules below. Slowly moving molecules that strike the surface row usually are reflected back. Faster molecules break through the surface; that is, they evaporate. —

convection, or radiation—the faster it will evaporate. Once it has been converted into water vapor, it acts like any other gas—if it is warm, it rises by convection. The heat that caused the evaporation is thus carried away.

Where did that heat come from in the first place? It came from something in the environment of the water. In the case we are considering, it came primarily from the bodies of animals. When an elephant or a pig has come out of the water or mud hole, its body is damp. Heat from the animal's body warms that thin layer of water, and as the water evaporates, the heat is carried away and the animal feels cooler. If an elephant has so little water available to it that it cannot bathe—perhaps a stream is very shallow, or a circus elephant has been given only a bucket of water—it will suck up water in its trunk and then spray it over its body. By giving its warm body a shower, the elephant has started the process of evaporation that will cool it. Once wet, an elephant's big ears provide a great deal of surface area on which evaporation of water can occur. On hot days, if there is no water available in its environment, an elephant may put its trunk into its mouth, suck up water from its own stomach and spray it over its body.

Some rodents use a cooling method comparable to the elephant's squirting himself with water from his stomach. They lick themselves all over

An elephant cooling himself by spraying his large but thin ears with water.

and coat their fur with their own saliva. Water in the saliva absorbs heat from the body and then evaporates. Dogs and cats also lick themselves in hot weather.

The rate at which water evaporates depends on its temperature and also on the amount of water vapor already present in the air. If there is very little water vapor in the air—as in deserts, for example—evaporation occurs more rapidly than if there is a great deal. If the air contains much water vapor, evaporation is slow. When the air is saturated with water vapor—that is, when it contains all the water vapor it can hold—evaporation ceases. We all know how uncomfortable a hot,

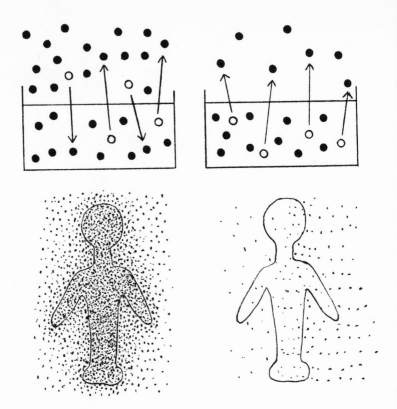

If the air is saturated with water vapor (left) the number of water molecules escaping from a body of water is equalled by the number of water molecules returning; that is, there is no evaporation. A human being is uncomfortable because perspiration does not evaporate. If the air is dry (right) evaporation occurs rapidly. If a breeze carries water vapor away (lower right) evaporation is even more rapid and more cooling.

muggy day is. That old expression, "It's not the heat, it's the humidity," is to a large extent true. When the air is saturated with water vapor, our perspiration does not evaporate but accumulates on our skin, and we feel hot, damp, and uncomfortable. On a drier, but equally warm day, we may feel perfectly comfortable because the evaporation of the water in our perspiration carries heat away from our bodies.

Wind has a cooling effect because it blows humid air away from the immediate vicinity of a wet animal and replaces it with drier air. As long as drier air keeps coming, the evaporation rate stays high, and the animal is cooled. This is a second reason—in addition to convection—why moving air usually has a cooling effect, whereas still air insulates.

4 · Behavior: Taking Care of the Young

Most young animals will grow best if their environment lies in a specific temperature range. In most cases the problem of the parents is keeping the young warm enough in a cool environment, but occasionally it is keeping them cool enough in a hot environment. In the case of mammals, very young animals are automatically kept warm inside the mother's body. After birth, in many species the young spend much time snuggled next to the bodies of one or both parents—perhaps in a sheltering den or burrow. In the case of animals that lay eggs, the eggs may receive little or no care— many fish, for example, do little more than lay their eggs in water of the temperature best for development—or they may receive a great deal of care—many birds provide elaborate nesting arrangements.

Incubating Eggs

Some egg-laying animals—especially birds and reptiles—build nests in which the eggs are kept warm. But the ways in which that warmth is provided varies. Sea turtles, which spend nearly all of their lives in water, come onto land only at egg-laying time. The female turtle chooses a spot on a beach, digs a hole, lays her eggs in it, covers them, and leaves. This is all the care she gives to her offspring. The beach receives sunshine by day, and the sand is warmed by the sun. The mother turtle has laid her eggs at a depth where they receive enough warmth but are not so near the surface that they are baked by the heat. There, under the sand, the embryos in the eggs develop into little turtles.

A female sea turtle lays her eggs in sand where the sun will warm them. Another turtle laid her eggs earlier.

Birds make a variety of nests from all kinds of materials—twigs, mud, leaves, even rocks. Most birds incubate their eggs and newly hatched chicks with the warmth of their own bodies. In some species only the female parent incubates, in some species only the male parent incubates, and in some species both share the task. If only one, the female parent, for example, sits on the eggs but her mate feeds her, then he is contributing to the warming of the eggs, because some of the energy stored in the food he brings her is converted to heat in her body, and some of that heat will be conducted to the eggs.

Incubating birds of many species develop special *brood patches* on their breast or abdominal area. When the eggs are laid, the parents lose their feathers in this area. At the same time, many small

A nest insulates young thrushes.

Capillaries are fine, microscopic blood vessels that branch from the smallest arteries (blood vessels that carry blood away from the heart). Each network of capillaries empties into one of the small veins (blood vessels that carry blood toward the heart). Because they are so small and so numerous, capillaries can lose a great deal of heat to surrounding tissues.

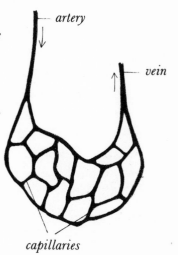

artery

vein

capillaries

blood vessels called *capillaries* develop in the skin of the brood patch and these bring warm blood close to the surface of the parent's body. Ducks and geese, which have no brood patches, pull out some of their own feathers and line the nest with them. In either case, the warm skin of the parent can be applied directly to the eggs or young chicks. With the insulation of a nest below and around them, the young birds are warm as long as one of the parents remains above them.

A few species have some interesting variations

on this general pattern. We will look at only a few examples, some that are about as far from the average bird nest as one could imagine.

Surprisingly enough, one of the coziest "nests" really isn't a nest at all, and the egg that doesn't have a nest is laid on the sea ice forming off Antarctica just as bitter winter comes to this already cold land. And what could be cozy about that? The answer is that after the female emperor penguin lays a single egg, she leaves it to go to feed for about two months, and her mate incubates it on top of his feet and under his brood patch. A special flap of skin on his abdomen covers the egg and protects it from

A male emperor penguin incubates an egg, which lies on his feet and is covered by a special abdominal flap. Young chicks are kept warm the same way.

wind. Completely surrounded by its father, the embryo in the egg is snug and warm.

Life for the male penguin is not so cozy at this time. For two months he stands, unable to feed, living on the fat deposits in his body. Penguins, you may recall, have a thick layer of blubber; and as this fat is used, it produces heat that warms both his own body and that of the chick developing inside the egg he guards.

A penguin huddle during a blizzard. Some penguin huddles contain thousands of birds.

When a blizzard strikes, the male penguins huddle together, thus reducing their total surface area exposed to the air. To get into the huddle, the male birds can only shuffle awkwardly, each taking care not to drop his egg. The birds within the huddle keep moving, those on the outside trying to get farther in where it is warmer, those that are forced to the outside gradually working their way back in. In this way no birds are on the cold, outer edge of the huddle for long.

About the time the chicks hatch, the female penguins, now well fed and carrying food in their stomachs, return and find their mates and off-spring. The male penguins now leave to feed, and for the next six or seven weeks, the females take over the task of sheltering the chicks between their feet and brood patches.

In hot climates, especially sunny ones, parent birds may have to keep their eggs cool rather than warm. Desert birds often build their nests in the shade, or they themselves stand in the sun and shade their eggs with their own bodies.

The Egyptian plover cools its eggs with water. The birds lay their eggs in sandy river banks. When the sun heats the sand to about 45°C (113°F) the parent birds begin making trips to the edge of the stream where they wet their breast feathers, then return to the buried eggs and allow the water to drop onto the sand over them. As the water evaporates it cools the eggs. The parents probably get some relief from the heat as the remaining drops evaporate from their feathers.

One of the most complex bird nests is that of the mallee fowl (or thermometer fowl) of Australia. These birds build such large, heat-producing nests that the nest itself provides all the warmth the eggs need and the parents do not sit on them at all. However, the parent birds do go to a great deal of trouble building the nest and keeping its temperature uniform for several months.

They begin by excavating a pit about a meter (1.09 yards) deep and then filling this with leaves, twigs, and other plant material. They keep collecting vegetation until they have a mound about a meter high. This they cover with a layer of sand that functions as insulation. The nest is warmed in part by the sun and in part by decay. The bacteria and fungi on the dead leaves and twigs cause the vegetation within the nest to decay—slowly at first,

A mallee fowl (thermometer bird) tests the temperature of the nest. The eggs lie in the upper part of a pile of rotting vegetation, and this is covered by a layer of sand.

then more rapidly. This produces heat, most of which remains within the mound because of the insulating layer of sand above. In a few months the temperature in the center of the mound reaches 34°C (93.2°F). The male bird then digs a hole down into the mound, his mate lays her eggs there, and he covers them with the mound material.

During the next six months, while the eggs incubate inside the nest, the weather changes from cool to hot and back to cool again. At the same time the rate of decay reaches a peak and then begins to decline; near the end of the incubation period, relatively little heat is produced by decay. Therefore, depending on the rate of decay and the outside temperature, the interior of the nest may begin to heat up or to cool down. Almost every day the parents test the temperature of the mound. They do this by sticking their beaks down into the mound and opening their mouths, which have temperature sensors inside them. The parents then make any necessary adjustments to the nest, cooling it if it is becoming too warm, warming it if it is becoming too cool.

Early in the incubation period, when decay is proceeding rapidly, the parent birds respond to high nest temperatures by removing some of the covering layer of sand. If, however, the nest should become cool early in the season, when decay is still producing some heat, the parents add sand to the insulating layer, thus conserving heat within the nest.

During the height of the summer season, when most of the vegetation within the mound has decayed away but the sun is shining brightly on the nest, the parents add more sand to the top of the mound, thus insulating the eggs from the heat of the sun.

Finally, when the weather is very hot in summer or very cool in autumn, the parents perform an operation that either cools or heats both the sand and whatever remains of the decaying vegetation and the eggs. The parents do this by removing most of the covering sand, spreading it over the ground, and, later in the day, replacing it on the mound. Whether the sand and the exposed nest are cooled or warmed by this operation depends on the time of day that it is done. In the heat of the summer the parents do it early in the morning; then both the spread-out sand and the exposed nest are cooled. They replace the cooled sand over the nest before the heat of the day comes. On the other hand, in the cool of autumn, this operation is performed in the warmth of the afternoon. Then both the spread-out sand and the exposed nest warm up in the heat of the sun, and the warm sand is replaced before the cool of the evening comes.

During the six months' incubation period, the nest does not need adjustments every day, but on days when a great deal of rearrangement is needed, the parent birds may work three, four, or five hours a day. As a result of all this work, the temperature inside the nest is kept virtually constant during the incubation period.

Honeybee Hives: Air-Conditioning and Central Heating

Animal homes built above the ground do not receive the benefit of insulation that soil provides. An above-ground home in summer is likely to become at least as warm as the air around it—perhaps considerably warmer—and in winter as cold as the air outside unless the occupants have some way of cooling and warming it.

During the summer honeybees keep their hives almost exactly at 35°C (95°F); this is the temperature that is best for their larvae. In the winter, honeybees cannot maintain the temperature of the hive that high, but they ordinarily do manage to keep the temperature of at least part of the hive between 20° and 30°C (68° to 86°F).

Honeybees build their hives in hollow tree trunks or other such cavities; some use boxes placed outside for their use by beekeepers. The bees maintain one opening as the entrance to their hive; they seal any others with wax. The wood of the tree trunk or box provides some insulation, for wood

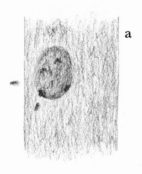
a

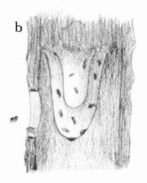
b

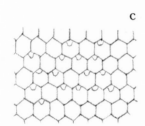
c

d

(*a*) *A hollow tree containing a beehive.* (*b*) *Combs hang down from the top of the hollow.* (*c*) *Detail of a comb showing the hexagonal cells in some of which worker bees have placed a drop of water.* (*d*) *Worker bee fanning her wings.*

consists largely of hollow dead cells, and each of these cells contains a small quantity of still air. However, wood alone is not enough to keep the temperature from rising inside the cavity when the hot summer sun beats down on it nor to prevent heat loss in winter.

Maintaining the hive temperature depends to a large extent on the collection of nectar from flowers. Nectar is mostly water but contains dissolved sugar. Some plants produce highly concentrated nectar—that is, with a high sugar content—others produce a dilute nectar. Some of the worker bees collect the nectar; they bring it to the hive and turn it over to other workers who fan their wings over it. This creates a draft that increases the rate at which water in the nectar evaporates. As the water evaporates, the sugar concentration rises and the nectar becomes honey, which is the main food of adult bees.

Ordinarily honeybees seek the most highly concentrated nectar they can find, for this reduces the amount of work that must be done in making honey. In hot weather, however, when the temperature in the hive begins to rise above 35°C, worker bees collect either water or the most dilute, watery nectar they can find. This they transfer to other workers, who distribute drops of liquid to various locations within the hive and spread it in a thin film over the walls. This creates a larger surface area of water than one large puddle would have. Still other worker bees create a draft by fanning their wings. This increases the rate of evaporation and cools the hive.

By regulating the amount of water brought into the hive, the bees maintain the temperature at almost exactly 35°C. As long as the worker bees can find water in their environment, they can keep the hive at this temperature during the hottest days of summer.

In autumn, as the environmental temperature falls, worker bees make fewer and fewer trips to flowers bearing nectar. Actually there are fewer flowers still alive then, and if all has gone well with the hive during summer, there is now plenty of honey stored away. As the environmental temperature continues to fall, the bees in the hive begin to cluster closer and closer together around the queen bee and the young bees. It is the queen that keeps the other bees together as a colony, and she is the only bee that lays eggs. Without her, the colony would break up.

As we have said before, all living things generate some heat, and although a single bee produces very little heat, a mass of 10,000 to 40,000 worker bees huddled together produces considerable heat. One honeybee alone in temperatures below about 7°C (44.6°F) cannot move, for its muscles are too cold to function; it will die unless

thorax

In cold weather worker bees form a cluster. The outermost bees form an outer shell by positioning themselves side by side with the hairs of their thoraxes meeting and forming an insulating layer.

the environmental temperature rises. But a tightly packed mass of thousands of bees conserves heat. The workers in the middle of the cluster generate extra heat by shivering their flight muscles, and those at the outside of the cluster form a shell that functions as insulation to the inner mass of bees. The bees in the outer shell face inwards, their heads toward the center of the mass and their abdomens pointing outward. Their thoraxes (the middle section of the body between the head and the abdomen) almost touch. Bee's thoraxes are covered with hairs, and the hairs on each bee in the shell mesh with the hairs on the adjacent bees. The many tiny air spaces among all the fuzzy thoraxes in the outer shell insulate the other bees from the cold winter air. In this way the center of the mass may be kept at about 30°C in winter, rarely less than 20°C and that only during the coldest part of winter. Even the bees in the shell stay warm enough to keep moving.

As the temperature around them rises or falls, the bees loosen or tighten the cluster a little. On warmer days, when they loosen up a bit, the cluster loses heat faster. On colder days, when they tighten the cluster, they conserve heat. The bees also exchange places within the cluster, those on the outside having a chance to move to the warmer center, those from the inside taking a turn on the outside. As long as the bees have access to a store of honey, they can convert some of the energy in it to heat. The sugar in the nectar that they collected last summer keeps the hive warm in winter. Without an adequate supply of honey the colony will perish.

Migration of Whales

So many kinds of animals move every autumn from places with cold winters to places with milder winters and then back again the following spring that we tend to think that escaping cold weather is the main function of migration. In fact, the weather is only indirectly responsible for the migrations of many species. Most species migrate because there is little food available in winter. Even rather small birds can withstand the cold of winter if they have plenty of food with which they keep their bodies warm. However, because the winter nights are long and winter days are short, very small animals do not have enough time during the short day to find the food they need to keep them warm during the long night. For such animals the possibilities are: storing food before winter comes, hibernation, and migration to a place where food is more plentiful.

There are a few species, however, in which the main function of migration is moving to a warmer climate. Whales are an example. In fact, in winter whales actually migrate to places with less food.

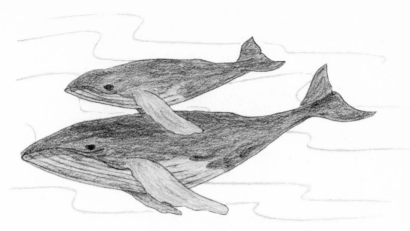

A female humpbacked whale with her calf.

Whales are among those aquatic animals that have only a relatively thin layer of hair, which provides almost no insulation from the chilling effect of water. Adult whales are insulated by a thick layer of blubber under their skins.

The feeding grounds of most whales are the coldest waters of the world—the arctic and antarctic seas. Life under water is different from life on land in more ways than just being wet all the time. In general, the colder the weather on land, the fewer plants are likely to be alive. Therefore, cold weather on land means hard times for many animals. In water, however, even though cold temperatures do slow growth somewhat, it doesn't get as cold as it does on land. Pure water freezes at 0°C (32°F), and ocean waters, which have some salt dissolved in them, freeze at only slightly colder temperatures. The coldest sea water has a temperature of $-1.9°C$ ($28.6°F$).

The colder the water, the more dissolved gases it can hold. Therefore, water below the freezing point holds much more carbon dioxide and oxygen than warm water. Because carbon dioxide is necessary for photosynthesis, very cold water can support more algae than warm water. Because oxygen is necessary for animals, cold water can also support more aquatic animals than warm water. Furthermore, all animals require food, and for sea animals algae are the basis of the food chain.

The humpbacked whales feed largely on a shrimplike animal called krill, which feeds on algae. Being very large, whales require a great deal of food. Humpbacked whales must spend most of their time where that food is most abundant, and that is in the cold waters of the extreme northern and southern parts of the oceans—the arctic and antarctic regions. The whales probably would never leave these regions were it not for one fact: young whales are born without blubber. Without the insulation of blubber, they would die in cold waters.

Each year, shortly before the time of birth, whales migrate from the cold, polar regions to warmer, tropical or semitropical waters. Here they give birth, and the young whales feed on their

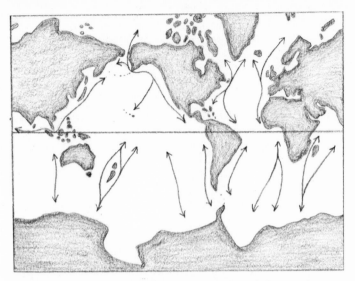

Migration routes of humpbacked whales of the northern and southern hemispheres.

mother's milk. With this milk they grow and produce their own blubber. The warm waters, which are comfortable for the young whales, offer relatively little food to the adult whales, who have to live largely at the expense of their blubber. However, after a few months, the whales return to their feeding grounds. As they proceed, they reach colder and colder waters, which contain more and more food. Adults and babies alike increase the thickness of their layers of blubber. By the time they reach their feeding ground, the young whales are sufficiently insulated against the cold of their new home waters.

5 · *What Goes on Inside*

So far we have only looked at those aspects of warming and cooling that we can see from the outside of the animal. However, a great deal of temperature regulation goes on inside the body. We will look at just a few examples.

More About Evaporation: Sweating and Panting

In a hot environment most homeothermic animals on land are cooled primarily by the evaporation of water that comes from within their bodies and is secreted and then evaporated into the air. The rate at which the body releases the water depends on the body's need to be cooled.

Two main ways a homeothermic animal can evaporate water are *perspiring* and *panting*. Relatively few animals perspire. Of these, human beings are the most profuse perspirers. Camels and horses also lose heat mostly by perspiring. Goats and sheep lose heat by both perspiring and panting. Dogs and cats lose heat mostly by panting; they have only a few sweat glands. Birds have no sweat glands and cool themselves by panting and by other ways of forcing air through their respiratory tracts.

Perspiration is a watery solution that originates in the blood. Water and some of the dissolved substances in the blood are forced out of the capillaries and into the *sweat glands* of the skin. Here the water in the perspiration—which has already been warmed by body heat—evaporates into the air, taking that heat with it. This cools the blood, and as the blood travels through the body it cools other parts by absorbing heat from them. When the

Sweat glands are long tubes in the skin. The deeper portion of each gland is twisted and covered by fine blood vessels called capillaries.

blood reaches the skin again, more water and heat are lost through the sweat glands. As long as perspiration forms and continues to evaporate rapidly, the entire body is cooled.

Because water is lost in perspiration, the body slowly becomes dehydrated unless the water is replaced by drinking. With an adequate supply of drinking water, a sweating animal can usually maintain its body temperature indefinitely in a hot, dry environment, but without access to water it cannot survive there long.

In very dry weather, the water in perspiration evaporates immediately after it reaches the air. No perspiration accumulates on the skin. In hot, humid weather, when evaporation slows down, however, moisture does accumulate on the skin. This is uncomfortable, but worse, without evaporation, the perspiration no longer cools. If the environmental temperature is 35°C (95°F) or higher, then in air saturated with water vapor, the heat produced by a resting human being cannot escape from the body as fast as the body produces it. Then the body temperature begins to rise above normal. For very active persons, who are producing even more heat, body temperature in saturated air may begin to rise when the environmental temperature is still as low as 30°C (85°F) or perhaps even a few degrees lower—it depends on how strenuous the activity and the size of the person.

Perspiring ordinarily is cooling only if the water comes out onto a bare or nearly bare skin. This is probably why human beings are among the "best" perspirers. A dense covering of fur prevents the movement of air away from the skin. The air near most fur- or feather-covered skin would become saturated with water vapor from perspiration very quickly on a hot day, and evaporation—and therefore cooling—would not occur on the surface of the skin.

Therefore, it is not surprising that most mammals whose bodies are covered with hair do not perspire. Neither do birds, with their covering of feathers. Camels are one exception to this general rule. Camels have a moderately thick, woolly coat over a skin that perspires. The air of the desert is so dry that even under its wool coat, the camel's perspiration evaporates as fast as it is produced—and a camel never seems to be sweaty. The camel's coat is necessary, for it acts as insulation; during daylight hours it keeps light and heat away from the animal. Some camel owners shear their camels for their wool. Shorn camels perspire more profusely than unshorn camels, for they require more evaporative cooling. Shorn camels require more drinking water than unshorn camels.

A great many animals—including dogs, cats, and sheep—cool themselves either completely or partially by panting. To most of us who look casually at a panting dog, it seems as if he is inhaling and exhaling through the mouth; and we assume, if we think much about it at all, that the evaporation that cools the dog takes place on his tongue, which ordinarily is wet. Actually, a panting dog usually inhales through his nose and exhales through his mouth, and nearly all the cooling evaporation occurs in his nasal passage.

The surfaces of a dog's nasal passages, like our own and those of other animals that breathe through noses, are moist, and so are the linings of the lungs and of the respiratory pathways that lead from the nasal passages to the lungs. The surfaces of these passageways are warm, and they are kept humid by the secretion of fluid from special glands in the nasal passage.

During ordinary, calm breathing, a dog inhales and exhales through his nose. If the dog inhales cool, dry air, then the air absorbs the water vapor that evaporates from the water on the lining of the nasal passages. By the time the air reaches the throat it has become considerably warmer and moister; this protects the delicate lining of the lungs from being exposed to cold, dry air. If the air is not saturated with water vapor by the time it reaches the lungs, it will become so there; it will also be warmed to body temperature if it has not already reached that point. When the air is exhaled through the nose, it is warmer and more humid

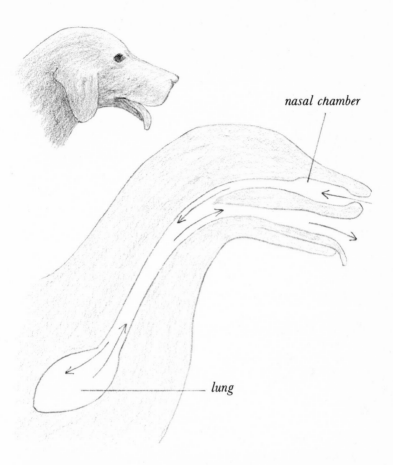

nasal chamber

lung

A dog usually pants by inhaling through the nose and exhaling through the mouth.

than it was when originally inhaled. This process causes some heat to be lost from the body, for each exhaled breath carries away some water vapor that evaporated from moist surfaces in the nasal pas-

sages. However, the loss of water and of heat during calm breathing is slight.

In dogs the walls of the nasal passages are bent
and folded; this increases greatly the total surface
area from which water can evaporate. When a
dog's temperature begins to rise, his rate of breathing increases, and he inhales through his nose and
exhales through his mouth. Both of these increase
greatly the rate of evaporation and the rate of
cooling. Each inhalation brings more dry air into

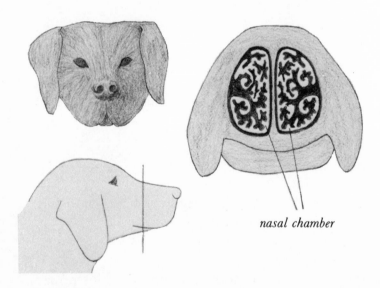

nasal chamber

*A dog's nasal chamber contains many convolutions that
increase greatly the surface area through which water can
evaporate.*

the nose, and exhaling through the mouth prevents moist air from the lungs from passing back through the nose. The nasal passageways are well supplied with blood vessels that carry warm blood to the nose and return cooled blood to the heart; from there it is carried to other parts of the body.

Only if this method of panting does not keep the body temperature normal do dogs begin to pant by inhaling and exhaling through both the nose and the mouth simultaneously. This brings some of the humid air back through the nose, but it also brings dry air through the mouth, and this increases somewhat the total surface area from which water can evaporate.

Like sweating, panting does not cool an animal when the air is saturated with water vapor.

Conserving Heat with Countercurrent Heat Exchanges

Although we speak of the normal body temperature of a human being or of some other species, the entire body is rarely the same temperature. Under ordinary conditions the central part of the trunk, neck, and head (the core of the body, which contains vital organs) maintain this normal or *core temperature*. The temperature of the skin approaches that of the environment, and there is a temperature gradient between the core and the skin. In hot weather the skin is warm, and the core temperature

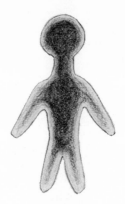

In a hot environment (left) the core temperature (dark) of a naked human being extends into the arms and legs, and the skin and tissues just below the surface are almost as warm. In a cold environment (right) the body conserves heat by maintaining the core temperature only around the vital organs. The skin is almost the temperature of the environment and will freeze if it becomes cold enough.

extends nearly to the skin. In cold weather the skin is cold, and the core temperature may not reach much farther than the core itself.

The parts of the body that are most likely to lose heat rapidly in cold weather are the long extensions such as legs, flippers, and some ears and tails. We have already seen that the ears of animals that live in very cold regions are usually shorter than those of similar animals living in warmer climates. Their legs are somewhat shorter, too, but there is a limit to how much these can be reduced before they become inefficient in locomotion. If an animal is to get about—and it must find food, for food is the source of much of the heat that warms it—it must put up with legs that look as if they were losers of heat rather than conservers of it. Inside these limbs, however, the blood vessels are arranged in such a way that some of the heat in the warm blood starting on its way toward the end of the leg passes into the colder, returning blood. Seals and whales have the same kind of arrangement in their flippers. In other words, although blood circulates in the limb, some of the heat never gets into the limb and so is not lost from it. This type of arrangement of blood vessels is a *countercurrent heat exchanger*. The heat from the warm blood flowing in one direction moves to a cooler blood flowing in the opposite direction. For heat to be exchanged efficiently, the two currents must be flowing very close to each other. This makes the temperature gradient between them steeper, and the steeper the temperature gradient, the faster heat is conducted.

In animals not adapted to the extreme cold of arctic and antarctic regions, the veins that return blood from the tips of the limbs do not lie particularly close to the arteries that take blood to the tips.

Warm blood is carried to the capillaries and there it loses some of its heat, and the cooler blood returns to the trunk where it is warmed again by the metabolism of the tissues there. In mild climates relatively little heat is lost from the limbs this way. In colder climates so much heat would be lost that it could not be replaced by metabolism, and the animal's core temperature would drop, putting it in danger of freezing to death.

(a) If a tube containing a hot liquid (dark) leaves a hot body and passes into a cool environment it loses heat and the cooled liquid (light) absorbs heat from the body to which it returns. (b) If the returning portion of the tube touches the outgoing portion, heat from the warm liquid warms the cool liquid before it returns; this is a countercurrent heat exchanger. (c) In many parts of many organisms, the arteries that carry blood away from the heart and the veins that return it lie at some distance from each other; heat is lost from the capillaries and the returning blood is cooler than blood that first reached the capillaries. (d) One type of countercurrent heat exchanger in animals of polar regions; a large artery is surrounded by many small veins, which it warms.

In this and the following illustrations, warm blood is shown as dark and cooled blood as light. The longer arrows indicate the direction of the flow of blood, and the short arrows show the major directions of the flow of heat.

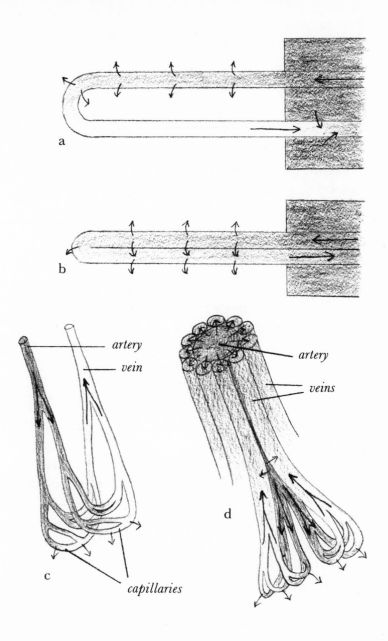

a

b

artery
vein

c

capillaries

artery

veins

d

In animals adapted to extremely cold climates, arteries and veins in legs or flippers run side by side, touching each other. Heat from the warm blood in the arteries is conducted across the thin walls of the blood vessels to the returning cold blood in the veins. This arrangement of arteries and veins is a countercurrent heat exchanger. Although a small amount of heat is lost from the limb, whatever heat was shunted from the arteries to the veins is heat that is conserved. The core temperature remains normal.

If so much heat is prevented from entering a limb in cold weather, what happens to the limb? It becomes cold. In cold winter weather, the temperature of the limbs of homeotherms adapted to arctic and antarctic climates falls to about 1°C (33.8° F). That is just above the freezing point of water and a little colder than the food in our refrigerators. What seems remarkable to us, who are accustomed to the comfort of boots and woollen socks in the winter, is that the wild animals of cold regions do not seem to be uncomfortable, even though their feet may be standing on snow at −40° C (−40° F) or colder. Some of this may be just a matter of becoming used to cold conditions. Hunting dogs and sheep dogs that spend their entire lives outdoors do not seem to mind standing on extremely cold snow, but pet dogs that live indoors begin to limp—apparently in pain—if they are required to go out for more than a few minutes in unusually cold weather.

What is, perhaps, even more remarkable is the fact that limbs with countercurrent heat exchangers do not freeze. If the temperature of the limb begins to fall lower than 1°C, more blood is allowed to circulate to the tip of the limb—just enough, but no more than necessary, to maintain a temperature of 1°C. This blood circulates through a system of small blood vessels that connect arteries and veins directly; it bypasses the capillaries. These small blood vessels are called *arteriovenous anastomoses* (which means a union of arteries and veins); they are also known as *AVAs,* for short. The AVAs are larger than capillaries, and so blood moves through them much more rapidly. As long as the temperature of the tissues in flippers or feet of arctic and antarctic animals remains above 1°C, the capillaries remain dilated (open wide) and the AVAs are constricted. When the temperature begins to fall below 1°C, the capillaries constrict and AVAs dilate. This brings a rush of warm blood through the limbs, and then the capillaries dilate again and the AVAs constrict. The temperature of the limbs is kept from falling below 1°C by repeated dilations of the AVAs. Dilations of AVAs do not occur any more frequently than is necessary to keep tissue temperature from falling below 1 °C.

There are at least two advantages to having

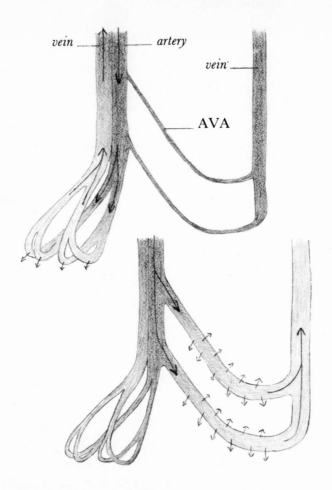

vein _____ ___ artery

vein ___

___ AVA

In many animals with countercurrent heat
exchangers there is an additional vein that is an
alternate route by which blood can return from the
limbs. This vein is connected to the artery by
arteriovenous anastomoses (AVAs). In the upper
drawing the capillaries are dilated and the AVAs
are constricted; this arrangement conserves heat

limbs as cold as possible without actually freezing. First the temperature gradient between the limb and the environment is not very steep, and so the heat that does reach the cold tissues of the limb is lost more slowly than it would be if the limb were warm. Second, if the limbs were too warm, the warm feet would melt their way downward through snow and ice.

Seals, which are insulated by blubber, have many AVAs, not only in their flippers but in the skin over the main part of the body. This skin, like wolf paws in winter, is at 1°C when the seal is in water or air at 1°C or colder. Spurts of warm blood into dilated AVAs prevent the flippers and skin from freezing.

Seals sometimes come ashore in warm weather, and then, with their thick insulating blubber, their body temperatures might rise dangerously if it were not for dilation of AVAs. With increased flow of blood in skin and flippers, seals radiate heat to the air and maintain normal body temperature.

but leaves the paws or flippers cold. In the lower drawing the capillaries are constricted and the AVAs are dilated. Because a great deal of blood flows through the AVAs enough heat is released to the tissues to keep them from freezing, but cool blood returns to the body.

Some arctic birds with webbed feet have AVAs in the webs that function the same way. They prevent the temperature of the feet from falling below 1°C in winter, and they prevent the bird's body temperature from rising above normal in warm weather.

Human beings have some AVAs, but not to the extent that polar animals do. We have them in our hands and feet, especially in the tips of fingers and toes; in elbows and knees; and in parts of the face including the nose. When these parts become cold, the capillaries constrict (saving heat), and occasionally the AVAs dilate. However, human beings are essentially tropical animals, and this system does not keep exposed hands, feet, and faces warm in bitter cold weather. Bare human hands, feet, noses, and ears will freeze under conditions that wolf paws and seal flippers can easily survive.

People who live in very cold climates do develop some degree of resistance to low temperatures. Eskimos, for instance, can usually work barehanded for longer periods in cold weather than can most other people; their bodies allow more warm blood to flow to their hands than do the bodies of most of the rest of us in similar weather. However, even Eskimos cannot keep their hands exposed to the bitter cold of the arctic winter for long without danger of freezing.

Perhaps the people who are most remarkable

for their resistance to cold are the Indians of the southern tip of South America and the nearby islands. Early European explorers in this area were amazed to find that the Indians went about practically naked in the snow and seemed not to suffer from it. On several occasions they saw naked women nursing naked babies while snow fell on them, and neither mothers nor babies seemed to feel that this was unusual. The most these Indians wore were loose fur capes, which they could shift around their shoulders to protect their backs or sides from cold winds.

It is true that the temperatures in the area do not fall much below freezing—nothing like the −50° C or lower than Eskimos sometimes experience—but the weather is always damp. The European medical researchers, who later studied these Alacalufe Indians, tried sleeping naked under the same conditions and spent the entire night shivering while the Indians slept undisturbed. The Indians, unlike most of the rest of us, maintain a high metabolic rate both day and night. Their body temperatures do not fall during sleep. Apparently this allows them the comfort that only thick blankets would give us under the same conditions.

Keeping a Cool Head: Another Use for a Countercurrent Heat Exchanger

If a countercurrent heat exchanger works by keeping one part of the body warm at the expense of cooling another, then it ought to be possible for a countercurrent heat exchanger to cool a part of the body as well. Dogs, cats, and several other animals that pant have countercurrent heat exchangers that prevent their brains from overheating in hot weather or during exercise.

You will remember that blood passing through the capillaries of the lining of the nasal passages of a dog is cooled as water evaporates there. The faster the animal pants, the faster that blood is cooled. This cooled blood returns to the heart and then is distributed to other parts of the body. But even before it reaches the heart it passes through a special countercurrent heat exchanger.

The small capillaries in the nasal passages unite into small veins, and these unite into somewhat larger veins. Then, just below the brain, these veins unite into one large, swollen structure called the *cavernous sinus.* From the cavernous sinus, other veins return blood to the heart. Arteries that carry blood from the heart to the brain enter the cavernous sinus. Here they divide into fine capillaries with very thin walls, and heat from the warm blood in the capillaries is conducted to the cool

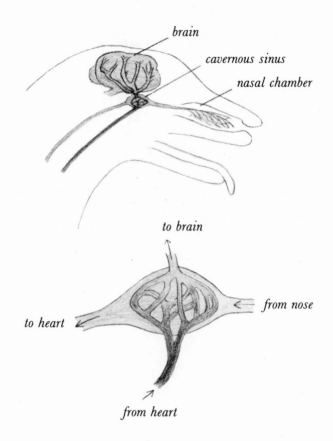

brain

cavernous sinus

nasal chamber

to brain

from nose

to heart

from heart

The countercurrent heat exchanger that cools the brain of the dog during violent exercise. Two separate currents of blood flow past each other in the cavernous sinus. Blood from the nose (cooled by panting) cools blood going to the brain.

blood from the veins. The capillaries and the cavernous sinus thus function as a countercurrent heat exchanger. The capillaries, containing the cooled blood, unite into arteries that go directly to the brain.

Thus during panting, evaporation cools blood in the capillaries of a dog's nose. This blood, carried by veins, cools the blood in the arteries going to the brain, and that blood cools the brain. The more a dog exercises, the more it pants, and the more its brain is cooled. During prolonged, violent exercise, a dog's brain temperature may fall while the temperature of the rest of the body is rising.

In some animals, it may be important to keep the brain warm when the environment is cold. It has recently been discovered that some sharks have countercurrent heat exchangers that warm their brains even though the rest of the body may be near the temperature of the water. (Sharks, like other fish, are generally regarded as poikilothermic animals.) Tuna and some other large fish have countercurrent heat exchangers that help to maintain the temperature of their swimming muscles above that of the water around them.

A Living Thermostat

It is important that the various processes of heat production, heat conservation, and heat loss be coordinated. If each occurs only at the appropriate time and at the appropriate rate, homeothermic animals can keep their body temperatures constant.

One part of the brain, called the *hypothalamus,* controls a number of body processes including those that are involved in temperature regulation. In this regard the hypothalamus functions something like a thermostat in a modern house. You set the thermostat for the desired temperature, which is called the *set point.* If, in winter, the temperature in the house falls slightly below the set point, the thermostat turns the furnace on, and then turns it off again when the set point is reached. In summer, when the temperature rises above the set point, the thermostat turns the air conditioner on, and then turns it off when the set point is reached.

The hypothalamus, like other parts of the body, is served by blood vessels, and in the hypothalamus are special *neurons* (nerve cells) that are sensitive to the temperature of the blood passing through the hypothalamus. So sensitive are these neurons that they can detect a temperature change of only a fraction of a degree. If they detect a drop in temperature, the hypothalamus secretes certain hormones and sends certain nervous impulses to other parts of the body where several processes are begun. These include increased production of metabolic heat, constriction of blood vessels in the skin (which also reduces sweating in those animals that

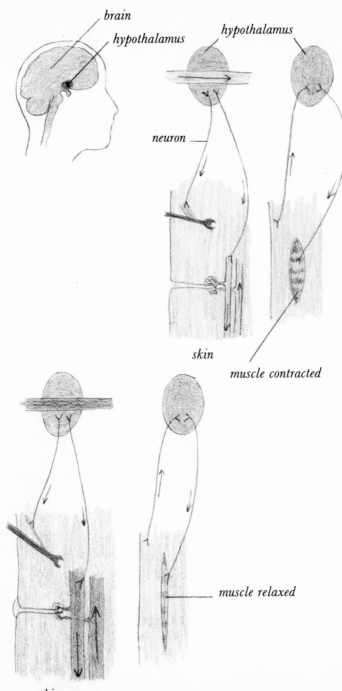

brain

hypothalamus

hypothalamus

neuron

skin

muscle contracted

muscle relaxed

skin

sweat), and contraction of pilo-erector muscles that raise hairs into an erect position (which increases the insulation value of the fur coats of animals, but gives human beings only "goosebumps"). These processes lead to production and conservation of heat.

If the neurons in the hypothalamus detect a rise in temperature of the blood, the hypothalamus secretes other hormones and sends other nervous impulses that bring about lowering of the metabolic rate, dilation of blood vessels in the skin (and increased rate of sweating), and relaxation of pilo-erector muscles (which decreases the insulation value of a fur coat). All these processes lead to loss of heat.

In addition to monitoring blood temperature, the hypothalamus receives nervous impulses from the skin, where there are some neurons sensitive to high temperatures and others sensitive to low temperatures. These neurons function as an early warning system. They inform the hypothalamus about changes in environmental temperatures before they affect blood temperature. If the skin is cold, stimuli from neurons sensitive to low tem-

The hypothalamus controls several processes that keep the body temperature constant despite changes in the environmental temperature. See text for details.

peratures reach the hypothalamus, and the hypothalamus sends other nervous impulses to muscles and causes them to shiver. Shivering is rapid and repeated contraction of muscles; it produces heat but accomplishes no physical work. If the skin is hot, stimuli from neurons sensitive to high temperatures reach the hypothalamus, and the hypothalamus sends other nervous impulses to muscles that cause them to relax, and so they cease producing heat.

In very small animals, which, because of their size, can lose or gain heat very rapidly, the hypothalamus is sensitive to very small changes in blood temperature. In larger animals, where the temperature of the blood changes more slowly because of the slower heat exchange with the environment, the hypothalamus is relatively more sensitive to changes in skin temperature.

Dogs have special neurons with endings in joints and muscles. When a dog exercises, these neurons function as another early warning system that body temperature may soon rise. Pressure on the neuron endings in joints and muscles changes as the dog moves, and impulses from these neurons to the hypothalamus cause the dog to begin panting before his body temperature rises.

All of these processes regulated by the hypothalamus usually keep the core temperature of homeothermic animals within a degree or two of their normal body temperatures. Only if the weather is extremely cold or extremely hot and humid, if the animal has been producing a great deal of metabolic heat by excessive physical activity, or if disease causes the hypothalamic system to fail, is the core temperature likely to vary from normal.

Part III

How People Keep
Warm & Cool

6·Clothing

Judging solely from the appearance of our bodies, one would think that human beings could live in only warm or hot climates. We have, for example, no fur protecting us in cold weather. In fact, a naked human being who is sitting quietly usually becomes uncomfortable when the temperature drops below about 28°C (82.4°F). An active, naked human being can endure somewhat cooler temperatures comfortably, but everyone must rest sometime. Most of us would die if we had to live without clothing or shelter at freezing temperatures, and we would surely die in the bitter cold weather of the polar regions.

Neither does the human body seem to be well adapted to very hot, very dry, sunny climates. With a body that perspires through nearly all of its surface area, a naked human being becomes dehydrated quickly in such a climate and dies in a matter of hours or days without a great deal of water to drink. Then, too, in a sunny climate, there is the problem of sunburn on exposed skin. This can be serious, especially for light-skinned people, who are likely to have sunburn and blisters if they remain in bright sunshine for a long period of time without first having gradually acquired a tan. Even if they do become tanned, light-skinned people are prone to skin cancer if they expose their bare skin to sunlight for long periods of time every day for many years.

Despite this susceptibility to the effects of extreme climates, the truth is that human beings have come to occupy permanently nearly all the land surface of the earth. Except for a few places where sufficient food cannot be raised—as for example in Antarctica or the driest of the world's deserts—human beings long ago came to live in relatively small, self-supporting groups throughout the world. One reason they could do this is that they learned to make clothes that would protect them from the harshness of their environments. In nearly every climate where there was sufficient food and water to support people, there were also materials that could be used to make clothing appropriate to that climate. People were also clever enough to produce clothing of appropriate cut and thickness to provide comfort.

This does not mean that all varieties of clothing devised by native peoples were those best suited to their climate. Like people today, ancient peoples were fashion conscious, and some styles of clothing were produced more for the sake of appearance than comfort. In addition, clothing sometimes is devised to protect from more than climate. Where there are many thorny plants, people may find thick leather clothing (like a cowboy's chaps) desirable, even though that clothing is not needed for warmth. Soldiers may have to wear uncomfortable clothing for purposes of camouflage or for protection from dangerous chemicals. In this chapter we will discuss a few examples of native clothing well adapted to a few climates. We are considering here clothing developed hundreds or thousands of years ago. Some of the descendants of the people who devised this clothing still wear the same type today, and some of them wear more modern dress.

Hot, Humid Climates

In the hot, humid, tropical rain forests (sometimes popularly called "jungles"), from a climatic point of view there is no need for clothing. In the humid tropics, perspiration does not evaporate readily, and clothing slows the rate of evaporation even more. As clothing becomes wet it clings to the skin and makes movement somewhat difficult and certainly annoying. People ordinarily can work most efficiently in such a climate with little or no clothing to hamper their movements.

Furthermore, perspiration contains dissolved salts and organic compounds. These are in low concentration, but they support the growth of certain bacteria and fungi, some of which produce odors that may or may not be offensive to the persons wearing the clothing or to their companions. In addition, these microorganisms produce acids and other chemical substances that cause cloth to disintegrate sooner than it would in a cooler climate.

Some native peoples wear very simple, light

South American Indians of different tribes. The man's feather "skirt" and body paint are for a celebration; ordinarily he would wear nothing.

clothing such as loin cloths or short skirts for the sake of modesty. Others feel no embarrassment about the human body, and they may wear necklaces, belts, and other items more for personal adornment than for any utilitarian function. Where clothing is worn by inhabitants of tropical rain forests, it often is made of dried grasses or other plant material. Such clothing can be replaced quickly when it wears out.

Tropical rain forests are dark, shady places, and many of the native peoples living there are

Two peasants from Hong Kong wear wide-brimmed hats that shade the face and shoulders.

dark-skinned. For these two reasons, they have no reason to protect themselves from sunshine by wearing clothing. Where forests have been cut down and people work exposed to the sun, they tend to wear lightweight, light-colored clothing that protects them from the sun. They may wear loosely woven, wide-brimmed hats that shade them from the sun. Air spaces in the woven material allow warm air from the body to escape as convection currents rise.

A Warm, Dry Climate

The ancient Egyptian civilization developed in the valley of the Nile River, which flows through land that is otherwise desert. The air, therefore, has a low humidity. Along the banks of the Nile River itself, there was plenty of water for drinking and for agriculture. The temperature, especially near the Mediterranean Sea, is warm most of the year; farther south it is hot.

The ancient Egyptians cultivated, in addition to several food plants, the flax plant from which they obtained long fibers that they wove into linen cloth. Depending on how it is woven, linen cloth can be relatively thick—as it is in some heavy, expensive tablecloths—or it can be quite fine and thin—as it is in delicate handkerchiefs. Linen, therefore, was ideal for clothing in a country where the temperatures varied from hot to mild.

Two ancient Egyptians as depicted on wall paintings.
The man, a worker, wears a short kilt as he picks figs.
The queen wears thin, transparent linen clothing.

Very fine linen is almost transparent. In hot, dry climates where perspiration evaporates just as soon as it reaches the surface of the skin, water vapor diffuses quickly through thin linen cloth. Even with moderate activity, clothing does not become sticky and cling to the skin. People who did hard physical labor that was likely to produce a good deal of perspiration simply shed their garments while working. White was the common color for clothing because it reflected sunlight, thereby reducing the amount of light that was absorbed and converted to heat.

Paintings and carvings that still survive on the ancient monuments show that the early Egyptians had rather simple clothing. Men wore a kilt that was wrapped around the hips and secured at the waist by a belt. The length of the kilt depended on the fashion of the times and the status of the person wearing it. It might end a little above the knees, a little below the knees, or even at the ankles. Women's clothing consisted of a tightly fitted wrap-around garment that usually extended from just above or just below the breasts to about the ankles. Shoulder straps held the dress in place.

A Hot, Dry, Very Sunny Climate

In the hot deserts of the world the air is dry and clear. Here water is scarce and can be obtained only at scattered sites called oases, which may be many miles apart. Many deserts are sandy or rocky, and because of the lack of water, the soil heats up quickly under the sun by day and warms the air above it. At night the heat of the ground radiates upward rapidly into the clear, cloudless sky and is lost to space. Therefore, the desert is hot by day and cold by night. People who live in such places must contend with both hot and cold weather and must do everything they can to conserve water.

The Bedouin Arabs are nomads that live in the deserts of Arabia and North Africa. The typical garments of these desert Arabs consists of loose, flowing robes. The robes cover the body from the neck down, and a head covering exposes only the face. Some Arab women wear veils that cover all of the face except the eyes; this is done primarily for modesty, but it also protects the face from sun and wind. Because clothing is loose, anyone can easily hold up a portion of a robe to protect the face if that becomes necessary. The hands are exposed while work is performed, but otherwise they are covered by the long sleeves of the robes. Leather-soled sandals protect the soles of the feet from the heat of the sand. Even though the upper part of the foot may be exposed during walking or running, a person can withdraw his feet under the robes while sitting or standing still.

From this description alone, the clothing of

A Bedouin Arab couple.

desert Arabs may appear to people from other climates to be hot, stuffy, personal "tents," but they really are well adapted to life in a hot, dry climate. Because the robes are loose, air moves freely between them and the body, and because the air is dry, perspiration evaporates quickly from the skin. With the robes open at the neck, at the hands, and at the feet, water vapor escapes quickly. However, in a land where water is scarce, it is not good to lose any more body water than is absolutely necessary. The thickness and the length of the robes protect the skin from direct sunlight and from direct wind, both of which are strong in the desert. The rate of evaporation of water from the skin is therefore lower than it would be if the person were naked or lightly clothed. The chance for sunburn is also reduced.

The outer woollen robe of Bedouin men is black; that of women is dark blue. At first these seem to be the wrong colors, yet they reduce the amount of sunlight that can penetrate through to the skin. If the robe were white, some sunlight would be reflected from one thread to another, and some light would reach the skin. In a thick, dark robe, however, the outermost threads absorb nearly all the light, and virtually none penetrates the robe. Then only the outer surface of the dark robe heats up appreciably. If the surface becomes much hotter than the air, a steep gradient is set up, and heat is lost quickly to the air. At the same time, the thickness of the robe insulates the wearer from whatever heat may develop at the outer surface. Robes of lighter weight are worn underneath.

At night, as the desert cools, the thick robes conserve body warmth. Sitting, the desert Arabs fold their legs and gather the hems of the robes around them. When they sleep, the robes function as blankets.

You may have noticed that in the description of these three hot-weather clothing styles developed long ago by native peoples, there was no mention of pants, both sexes wearing what amounts to skirts. Furthermore the garments either had no sleeves or, in the case of the Arab robes, only very loosely fitting ones. In other words, the spaces between the legs and under the arms were free of clothing that would inhibit the free flow of air and that would accumulate perspiration.

A Very Cold, Snowy Climate

The clothing of Eskimos and of other people who live in very cold climates is different. Eskimos have the problem of inhibiting the flow of air around the body, for moving air would carry heat away from the body very quickly, and this cannot be tolerated in cold climates. Eskimos solved this problem by making their clothes of skins of caribou, fox, and other animals with warm fur; the many small insulating air spaces among the hairs prevent moving air from reaching the body. The clothes are cut so as to fit the major contours of the body—that is, with sleeves and legs.

The traditional outdoor clothing of Eskimos consists of trousers, a parka (a long-sleeved shirt with a hood), boots, and mittens. In summer, these consist of a single layer of clothing worn with the fur side out, and the hood and mittens may be omitted. In the winter, Eskimos wear a double layer of clothing, the outer layer with the fur side

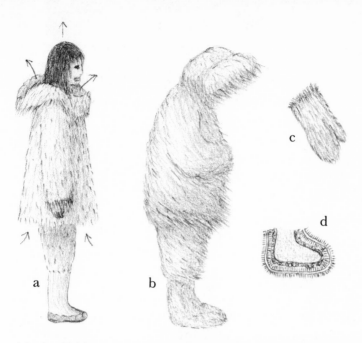

(a) *An Eskimo man in moderately cold weather wears one layer of clothing and allows air to move upward in his loose parka.* (b) *In a blizzard he wears a double layer of furs and protects his face with the ruff of his parka hood. In very cold weather he would withdraw his hands into his parka.* (c) *Fur mittens.* (d) *Boots of a double layer of furs are lined with dry moss or grasses.*

out, the inner layer with the fur side in. The inner layer functions as warm underwear and socks and provides a thick layer of insulation next to the skin. A strong wind might penetrate air spaces among the hairs of the outer layer of clothing, but the air spaces among the hairs of the inner layer are free from disturbance.

Because their feet walk on the surface of the cold ground and lose heat to it by conduction, they need extra insulation. Eskimos stuff their boots with dry mosses or grass.

So good are the insulating qualities of this clothing that the body heat of a physically active Eskimo is retained within the clothing and surrounds the body with a tropical environment. It is dangerous, however, for a person wearing such clothing to become warmed to the point that perspiration forms and soaks into the clothing, for when water fills the air spaces, the clothing loses its insulating qualities, and heat is lost rapidly to the environment. If this happens, the temperature of the furs falls, and water freezes in the clothing and further chills the body.

Eskimo clothing is constructed so that the wearer can control the amount of body heat that escapes to the environment before he begins to perspire. The parka is a moderately loose garment with a drawstring at the bottom that can be tightened around the hips for warmth, but that can be loosened to allow air to enter whenever the wearer feels he is about to become too warm. The hood of the parka, which has a thick ruff that protects the face from cold winds, can be thrown back, baring the head and allowing air to move upward within the parka. Long mittens, which when fitted over the sleeves of the parka prevent air from entering the sleeves, can be removed to allow air to enter. By any of these adjustments of clothing, the Eskimo can lose some of his body heat to the environment. If he needs to be still cooler, he removes the outer clothing. It is important that he know enough about how his own body reacts to physical activity that he can begin to make these arrangements before he begins to perspire noticeably. When he feels that he has cooled the air within his clothing sufficiently, he then begins to reverse the process by returning any clothing he has removed, tightening the parka, covering his head with the hood, and returning the mittens to his hands. The dry mosses or grasses in the boots are usually changed each day because they slowly absorb perspiration.

If furs do become wet, either from perspiration or from some other source, the best way to dry them is to remove them, throw them outside until the water in them freezes, and then beat the clothing to remove the particles of ice. Fur deteriorates if it is dried by holding it in front of a fire to cause the water to evaporate.

During part of the winter Eskimos may experience temperatures of $-40°C$ ($-40°F$) or $-50°C$ ($-58°F$) or even colder. In such bitter cold weather, especially if the wind is strong, mittens, no matter how thick, do not provide sufficient protection to the hands. Because the Eskimo parka fits loosely, the wearer can, when he feels his hands becoming cold, withdraw his arms from the sleeves of the parka and bring them against his chest where the temperature is warmer.

Caribou skins are a favorite for Eskimo clothing because the hollow hairs provide excellent insulation. When garments must be waterproof, however, the outer layer is made of sealskin. Sealskin is not so warm as caribou skin, but it may be a lifesaver if it prevents a hunter from becoming soaked with water while hunting seals or pursuing whales.

7 · Homes

Clothing alone does not always provide sufficient protection against weather. People also require some shelter against extremes of temperature. Just as the early inhabitants of the many parts of the world devised styles of clothing that were suitable for the climates they found there, so they also made homes that would keep them as comfortable as possible.

Grass Huts

In tropical rain forests, where the temperature is high the year around, there is no need for shelter to keep warm. Rain is common, however, and that makes at least a roof over the head necessary. Native huts in such a climate usually consist of a few poles that form a framework on which a thatched roof is laid. Thatch is plant material, such as leaves or straw (usually the stems of grasses or some other plants after the seeds or fruits have been har-

A pygmy hut from central Africa (above) is made of a framework of saplings covered by leaves. Such a hut is rather humid inside. A South American Indian hut from the Amazon region is airier; the Indians sleep in hammocks.

vested). The sides of the building may have walls made of leaves, straw, or branches. These are usually arranged thickly enough to provide privacy, but loosely enough to allow air to enter the building more or less freely. Ventilation is necessary to keep the hut as cool as the weather will allow, for the humidity is high in rain forests and a closed building soon becomes very uncomfortable.

Grass huts do not last long, for plant materials decay quickly in hot, humid climates. However, they are also easy to make, and the materials are always near at hand. The simplest huts require only an hour or two to construct.

Some inhabitants of tropical rain forests, the Indians of Brazil, for instance, sleep in hammocks of twine made from plant fibers. By knotting the twine to form a netting, they make a very lightweight hammock that holds the sleeper well above the damp ground and reduces the chances of his being bothered by small, ground-dwelling animals. The hammock also allows cooling breezes (if there are any) to strike the sleeper on all parts of his body. Indians also use hammocks for lounging during the day.

Tents of the Desert Arabs

In the broad expanses of sandy desert where the Bedouin Arabs live, there are no trees with which to build substantial dwellings, nor would such buildings be desirable for nomadic people who are always on the move in search of water and grazing land for their animals. Instead, these desert Arabs live in tents.

Upon arriving at a camping place Arabs begin to assemble their tents by first placing tent poles in a rectangular pattern. Over these they arrange two long woollen curtains so as to form a roof and 3 walls. The open side of the tent faces away from the wind. The interior of the tent is divided by additional curtains into as many compartments as

A Bedouin Arab tent. The upper drawing shows the tent poles and one curtain that forms the roof and the upper part of the rear wall. The lower drawing shows the curtains that form the lower part of the walls and the dividing wall that separates the men's and women's compartments.

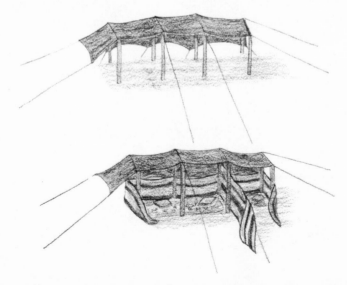

desired. There are usually at least two compartments, one for men and one for women. The lower
edge of the lower curtain is secured by a covering of
sand. Breezes enter the tent through the space between the two curtains and leave through the open
side.

The tent roof provides shade from the sun by
day and prevents radiation of heat to the open sky
at night, when the desert becomes cold. If camp is
made early enough in the day—while the ground is
still hot—blankets can be spread on the ground.
This helps to conserve the heat below them. This
heat is conducted upward slowly through the night
and warms the sleeper.

Caves, Natural and Artificial

One material used for shelter by people in many
climates is the earth itself. Some of our early ances-
tors used natural caves if they were available, and
there are still people today who use them.

One advantage of a cave is that, because earth
changes temperature more slowly than air, a cave
is usually cooler than the outside air on a hot day
and warmer than the outside air on a cold day or a
cold night. Even a shallow cave shows some of this
effect, but a cave that extends deep into the earth
has a constant temperature the year around. The
temperature might be about 13°C (55.4°F), warm

A cave is one of the oldest types of dwelling. It holds a constant temperature.

enough to sleep comfortably under blankets. If the cave has two openings, a draft of air most likely will keep moving from one opening to the other. Then a fire can be lit in the cave for warmth or cooking. Caves are particularly comfortable in hot, dry climates where there is little danger of flooding and where their coolness is appreciated.

In a few places, people have made their homes by actually carving caves out of the earth. One such place is an area of Turkey formerly called Cappadocia. Millions of years ago volcanoes erupted here, and the lava, together with ash, covered the countryside in thick layers. This volcanic deposit is called *tuff.* Tuff is a soft stone, and after the volcanic activity stopped, wind and rain wore much of it away. What remains of the tuff today stands in the form of huge cones and pinnacles; these formations are called the Cones of Cappadocia.

When people discovered that it was very easy to cut into the volcanic tuff, they began carving homes out of the cones. Over the centuries, some of the larger cones have been turned into "apartment houses." Smaller cones are single-family dwellings. Some rooms serve as barns, pigeon roosts, or storehouses.

Like natural caves, rooms in the cones change temperature much more slowly than does the outside atmosphere. Such homes last many years and

The Cones of Cappadocia from which many generations have carved their homes.

can be enlarged simply by carving another room out of the rock. The cones do erode slowly in the wind and rain, and eventually they must be abandoned, but usually not until at least a few generations of people have lived in them.

Mud and Brick: Homes in Hot, Dry Climates

In the ancient Middle East and in other hot, dry climates where mud was available along riverbanks and where rain was infrequent, people often built mud homes. Even in prehistoric times people built the walls of their homes by mixing straw with wet mud and spreading a thin layer either on the ground or on a foundation of stones. A day later, when this had dried in the sun, they added a new layer and allowed it to dry for a day. This was repeated until the walls had reached the desired height.

To make the roof, people laid poles made from young trees or from tree branches from wall to wall. They covered the poles with straw topped off by a final layer of mud. The roofs were flat, not peaked as they are in places where rain or snow are common. As long as there was little rain, there was little danger of its accumulating on a flat roof.

Sun-dried mud holds its shape as long as it remains dry, but it softens in water and eventually washes away. Therefore, mud houses were suitable

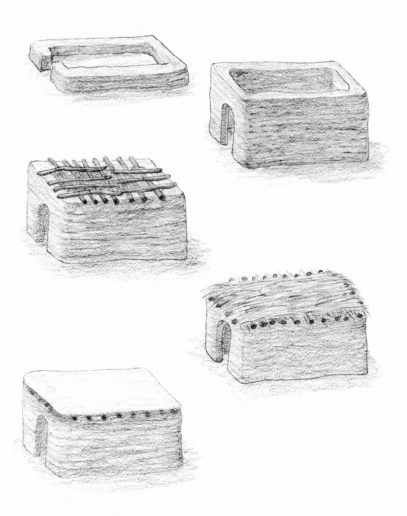

The making of an ancient type of mud hut in the Middle
East. The walls are made of repeated layers of sun-dried
mud and straw. The roof was made by crisscrossing
saplings or branches and covering them with grass and
mud.

only in very dry climates. Later, people made bricks dried in a furnace. These were resistant to the effects of water, and the houses made of fire-dried bricks lasted much longer than sun-dried mud huts.

People who lived in mud or brick homes were surrounded by earth, though not as thick a layer of it as people who lived in caves. Mud and brick homes heat up slowly and cool slowly. Therefore, during the day the temperature inside usually is cooler than outdoors. At night, the walls radiate their heat and keep the house warmer than the outdoors.

In very hot climates, however, such houses may become uncomfortably hot as the summer progresses, for the walls gradually become warmer

A brick house in a modern village in Egypt. The roof is protected by a low wall that provides privacy for social gatherings and sleeping.

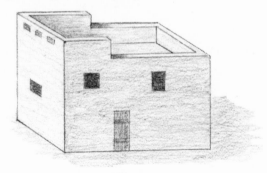

every day and radiate some of their heat inward both day and night. For this reason, the flat roofs were used after sundown for social gatherings and as bedrooms. Open to the cloudless night sky, the roofs and the people on them radiated their heat upward into space, and breezes helped to cool them. With little rain, people did not have to worry about their sleep being disturbed by a shower.

Cooling Domes and Towers: Simple Air Conditioners

Not all buildings of the desert areas in the Middle East are flat-roofed. Some buildings have domes that add much to their beauty, but the domes also cool. When air flows over a dome, it moves faster than when it flows over a flat surface. This makes a domed roof somewhat cooler than a flat roof.

The faster air moves, the lower is its pressure. When there is a difference in air pressure, air under high pressure moves toward a low-pressure area. Therefore, if the dome has an opening in it, and if some of the windows or doors are left open, air moving near the ground and entering the windows or doors will rise upward inside the building toward the area of low pressure slightly above the dome. This creates a breeze in the building in hot weather.

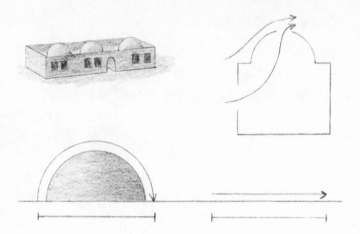

Air traveling over a dome has a farther way to go than over a comparable piece of flat roof. The air moving over the dome travels faster than air over a flat roof and therefore has a lower air pressure. If the dome has an opening in the top, a breeze is drawn through it if the building has another opening.

If the occupants can afford it, they have a small pool of water immediately below the dome. In a dry atmosphere water evaporates quickly, and the cooling effect of evaporation lowers the temperature of the air in the building. To insure even faster evaporation, some people have fountains that spray water into the air; this increases the surface area of the evaporating water.

Other buildings may have wind towers in place of domes—or in addition to them. The wind towers are taller than the buildings and connect

A cooling tower. The upper drawing shows the direction of flow of air through the tower and the house whenever there is a breeze. Because the tower has openings on all four sides (only two shown here) it can catch wind coming from any direction. Air descending through the tower pushes air through the building. The same direction of flow occurs early in the morning when there is no wind. The lower drawing shows the direction of flow of air in the afternoon, evening, and early part of the night when there is no breeze. Air rising in the tower pulls air through the building.

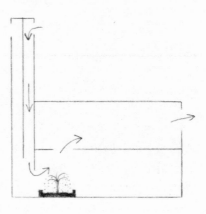

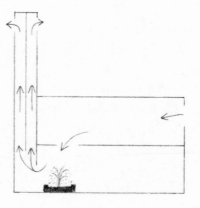

with them through doors in the basement and the main hall on the first floor. How the towers work depends on the environmental conditions at the moment. They either push or pull air through the building.

The interior of a tower is divided into separate shafts, and if there is a wind, no matter from what direction it comes, it hits an inner partition and is directed downward through one of the shafts. The breeze moves downward inside the tower, into the building, and out its open windows. Many buildings with wind towers have a pool and perhaps also a fountain just inside the door connecting the tower and the basement. Evaporation of water cools the entering breeze.

In some cases the tower stands a distance away from the building and is connected to it by an underground tunnel that is cooled by contact with the cooler ground a few meters below the surface. If any subterranean water seeps into the tunnel walls and evaporates there, air moving through the tunnel is cooled still more.

If there is no wind, then early in the morning, the bricks of which the tower is made have gradually cooled during the night are now cooler than the air, which is being warmed in the sunlight. The air in the tower loses heat to the bricks, and the cooled air, being heavier than warmer air, sinks in the tower and flows into the building and out its open windows or doors.

As the day progresses, the bricks in the tower become heated in the sunshine, and they lose heat to the air in the tower. If there is still no wind, the hot, lighter air begins to rise in the tower, and this pulls air from the building into the tower. This air is not cool, but it does provide a breeze in the building.

Because bricks lose their heat slowly, they are still radiating heat during much of the night, and on calm nights the air warmed by the bricks continues to rise in the tower. This pulls air from the building into the tower, and as a result, cool night air flows into the open windows or doors.

By opening and closing doors and windows throughout the building, the occupants can control the degree of cooling of each room. By closing doors between the tower and the building they can close off the tower and rely solely on the cooling effect of a dome and pool if the building has these. Where winters are cold, the openings in domes and the doors between towers and buildings must be closed to prevent cold air from entering the buildings.

The Sod House: Another Earthen Home

When pioneers settled on the Great Plains of the United States in the middle of the nineteenth century, they were faced with a problem that earlier settlers in the eastern states never had. These prairies were a vast grassland with almost no trees except for a few along stream banks. It was impossible to build frame houses or log cabins because there was almost no wood.

Yet the need for a sturdy shelter was great. This area experiences wide variations of temperature. For most of the settlers, whether from the eastern states or from Europe, the summers were hotter and the winters were colder than anything they had ever experienced. In this vast expanse of flat land, there was no shelter from winds that blew unchecked. Blizzards raged across the land in winter, and the summers could be swelteringly hot. For most settlers, imported wood from eastern states was much too expensive, and so they made do with the one material there was plenty of: *sod.*

Sod is the upper few inches of soil in which grow the roots of grasses and other prairie plants. The roots in prairie soil that had never been plowed held the rich earth together so well that it can be cut into pieces that held their shape with no further treatment. A special plow was devised that cut long ribbons of sod no more than about 60 centimeters (2 feet) wide and about 10 centimeters (4 inches) deep. The ribbon, which was as long as the settler wanted to make it, was cut into smaller pieces called sods. The sods were then stacked like bricks to make the walls of the house. Unlike a

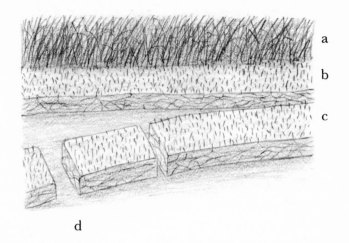

a

b

c

d

First steps in the construction of a sod house. If the grass is tall (a) it is mowed (b). The earth containing the grass roots is cut into long ribbons (c) and these are cut into smaller, brick-shaped pieces called sods (d). The walls of the house are formed by laying a double thickness of sods in a brick-wall type of arrangement.

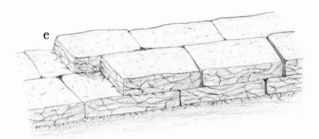

e

brick wall, however, there was no mortar; the sods were merely placed grass side down. If the grass was tall, it may have been mowed before cutting the sod. The walls were 2 or 3 sods thick, making a total wall thickness of about 3 feet. Wood was used only for doors, the casements of doors and windows, and the roof.

The roof, which was slanted to shed rain, was made by first placing several wooden beams across the walls so as to span the house from side to side. On these were placed either cut lumber or the trunks of sturdy saplings. Whatever was used, it had to be strong enough to support additional sods, which would become heavier from soaking up water during rains or bearing the added burden of snow in the winter. But before the sods were laid, the roof was covered with cut grasses and then, to waterproof the house, a layer of gypsum plaster or alkali clay was usually added. The sods were the final covering.

There were usually two layers of sods on the roof with the upper one right side up. The grasses in them usually were not mowed. Still alive, the roots continued to grow and extended from sod to sod binding them all into one piece. As the stems and leaves grew upward, they shaded the roof itself and so prevented it from heating up under the summer sun as modern roofs do. In addition, the living roots in the roof absorbed rain

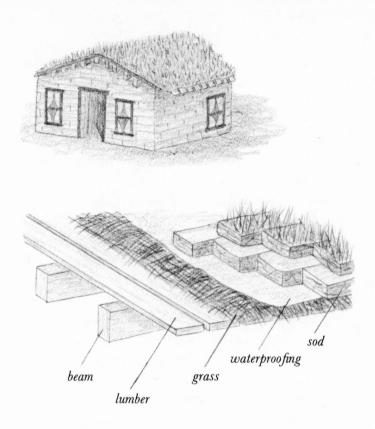

A sod house and the details of its roof.

water. The water travelled upward in the plants
and evaporated from the leaves. The evaporation
cooled the air immediately above the sod. All this
kept the roof cool and so helped to keep the house
cool in summer. Heat could penetrate the thick sod
walls only very slowly. Most of the heat that did
enter came in through the doors and windows, but

with the natural air-conditioning provided by the sod roof and the insulation provided by the walls, the sod house was comfortable most of the summer.

More important than summer comfort was winter comfort in a land with cold winters. Here, again, the sod solved much of the problem. Sod houses were easier to heat than frame houses or log cabins, for the house was its own insulation. The roof, with the remains of last summer's grasses, caught snowflakes, and an extra layer of insulation in the form of a blanket of snow covered the roof. Even in the Great Plains blizzards, sod houses could be kept cozy, while wooden houses, which lost heat quickly through the walls, were warm only in front of the fireplace. The matter of good insulation was doubly important where there was no wood or coal to burn for fuel. In the early days on the plains, the fuel was the dried manure from bison ("buffalo chips") or, later, as the bison disappeared, from cattle. In addition, the sod house was virtually fireproof, whereas a wooden building could burn if sparks flew from a roaring fireplace.

The main disadvantage of a sod house lay in an improperly waterproofed roof. During a heavy rain, such a roof would, at the very least, leak, much to the annoyance of the occupants. If the rain were prolonged, chunks of sod or even the entire roof would fall into the house.

Some sod houses still stand on the Great

Plains, but most of them are kept only for their historical interest. Only a few still serve as homes.

Igloos: Snug Homes of Snow

In the far north of Canada, beyond the tree line, where the ground is frozen much or all of the year, there are no trees and no sod with which to make houses. For temporary winter homes, the Eskimos who settled in this bleak land used the material that most of us would at first seek to avoid in cold weather: snow. Remember, however, that the air spaces in snow give it good insulating properties. The Eskimos used it to make a dome-shaped snow house called an *igloo*.

The first step in constructing an igloo is selecting the right kind of snow. It cannot be packed down too hard, for then the air spaces will have been squeezed out of it, and it will not be good insulation. On the other hand, it cannot be very light, fluffy snow, for that kind of snow will not hold its shape when cut into blocks.

When they found snow of just the right consistency, Eskimos cut blocks a little less than a meter (about 3 feet) long and about 60 centimeters (2 feet) high and 15 centimeters (6 inches) thick. The opposite sides of the blocks were not parallel but were tapered a bit so that when they were placed side by side they would form a circle, and when one

sleeping
platform

Steps in the construction of a snow igloo.

162

block was placed on another they would curve inward, forming a dome. The first two or three blocks had their tops cut off diagonally, so that when the first circle of blocks was completed, it would be continuous with the second layer, which, when it was completed, would be continuous with the third layer, and so on. The entire igloo consisted of a single row of snow blocks spiralling up from the base to the center of the dome. Loose snow was stuffed into any chinks between the blocks. A small opening was left at the top for ventilation. This could be filled with dry mosses or grasses if that was desired or with one last snow block cut to fit the opening.

The entrance to the igloo was a tunnel cut through the snow lower than the floor of the igloo and roofed over with blocks of snow. The tunnel either had a right-angle bend or was T-shaped to prevent winds from entering the igloo, but it did allow air to circulate from the tunnel to the ventilation hole at the top. In a T-shaped tunnel the opening at the upwind side was closed. The tunnel also served as a cold-storage room where extra meat would stay frozen all winter long.

A properly made igloo was very strong and was not likely to collapse even if people or animals walked on it. The thick snow blocks with their many air spaces among the snowflakes provided insulation from cold winds. Eskimos often heaped additional snow around the base of the igloo, and any fresh snow that fell added more insulation.

Inside the igloo, opposite the entrance, a sleeping platform was built of snow. This occupied more than half of the igloo. It served as both bedroom and living room. The platform was covered with two layers of blankets made of caribou skins. The lower skin was placed hair side down, the upper one hair side up. The two layers insulated a sleeping person from the snow beneath. This was important not only for the immediate comfort of the Eskimos, but it also protected the snow platform from the heat of the sleeper's body. If the snow were to be warmed by a person's body, it would melt.

Eskimos traditionally slept naked, with more caribou blankets above them, the lowest one with the hair side down. In other words, the sleeping Eskimo was protected from cold indoors the same way he was protected outdoors, with the insulation of animal hairs all around his body.

The remaining floor space in the igloo was lower than the sleeping platform but higher than the tunnel. Here is where one or more lamps were lit. These lamps burned seal blubber, and they provided both light and heat. Because warm air rises, a gentle flow of air moved from the tunnel, past the buring lamps, and then out the ventilation hole at the top of the igloo. This kept the air in the igloo fresh, and because it passed the lamps it was always warm.

The lamps were also used for cooking, and the heat from the lamps together with the heat produced by the bodies of the occupants, warmed the igloo to a room temperature that might reach 25°C (77°F) or more. Eskimos sometimes insulated the igloo walls from the heat of the lamps by arranging a layer of animal skins on the inner surface. Then if a little of the snow melted, the drops of water ran down the inner curved wall and did not drip onto the occupants of the igloo.

It was so warm inside an occupied igloo that Eskimos coming in from the outdoors ordinarily removed most of their clothing immediately, leaving on only their inner trousers and socks. This prevented them from soaking their furs with perspiration and perhaps ruining them.

Despite its strength and the snug warmth it could provide, the igloo had two drawbacks. One was that it was small, perhaps only ten or twelve feet across, and it could become very crowded. When a family was large, sometimes two igloos were built close to each other with a connecting tunnel. The other, and more serious, drawback was that an igloo could be only a temporary home. Because of the heat produced inside, an igloo began to melt in spring even before the outdoor temperature rose to the melting point of ice. Then the inhabitants had to begin to make their summer homes. These usually were tents of a double layer of caribou skins hung on wooden poles or the rib bones of whales.

Igloos are not much in use today, especially not as family homes. Most Eskimos live in buildings of modern construction made from wood and other materials imported from farther south. Hunters who travel far enough to spend the night away from home may have to build a small igloo for shelter, but now that snowmobiles have reached the arctic, even that is not often necessary.

The Japanese Bath

Except for its northernmost islands, Japan has a rather mild climate most of the year. In the south the winters are mild, and in central Japan most winters are only moderately cold.

The traditional Japanese house was made of bamboo, and the inner walls were often made of heavy paper. This was a good choice in a land that has frequent earthquakes, for if a house collapsed with a family still inside it, these lightweight materials would cause far less injury than would heavy logs or stones or bricks. These houses were not well insulated, however, and did not have central heating. Even during mild winters, the inside of a house could become chilly, especially at night. Individual rooms could be kept warm with the heat from hot coals in a small portable brazier, but the Japanese devised an additional method of keeping warm in the evening: the Japanese bath.

Each house has a bathroom which is exactly that: a *bath* room. It is only for bathing. The tub, which may be sunken into the floor, is filled to the top with water heated from below. Because water cools so slowly, there is usually no need to keep the fire lit once the desired temperature is reached. The tub may be partially covered to conserve heat. Ordinarily, the water is so hot that anyone who has never had a Japanese bath before is certain to feel that he is being boiled to death as he enters the water.

A Japanese bath.

Before actually entering the tub, the Japanese first wash thoroughly with soap and water. Using a bucket, they scoop water out of the tub and wash with that; no one washes in the tub itself. Then they use another bucket or two of clean water from the tub for rinsing. There is a drain in the bathroom floor, and the floor slants slightly toward it. All the wash water and soap run down to the drain in the floor; no used water goes back into the tub. Only after they feel completely clean and rinsed do the Japanese enter the tub. There, in clean, hot water up to their necks, they relax for a while.

The human body reacts to being submerged in hot water as it would to hot weather. Muscles relax, and the blood vessels in the skin dilate, bringing a great deal of blood to the surface. However, because the body is surrounded by hot water, it does not cool. Any perspiration formed cannot evaporate under water. Rather, because the water is hotter than the human body, heat moves into the body. For the time a person relaxes there, body temperatures rises a degree or two.

When bathers emerge from the tub, they dry themselves and then dress, donning a series of kimonos. The first is a lightweight cotton kimono that probably will be used as sleepwear later in the evening. Over this is a heavier kimono, and perhaps another over that. The outer kimono may be of heavy silk or wool. All these layers insulate the body, now slightly warmer than normal, from the cool air in the other rooms of the house, where the family may spend a social hour or two. Their bodies, still with dilated blood vessels, continue to release heat for a long time, but the heat is held within the layers of kimonos. It may take a few hours for their bodies to cool, and before then it probably will be time to go to bed under a couple of thick comforters.

The Japanese wash before entering the tub to keep the hot water as clean as possible, because everyone in the family and any guests in the house use the same water. They may take turns, or, in some families, all bathe together. Guests ordinarily bathe first, when the water is hottest.

By this method, an entire Japanese family might keep warm on chilly nights by using only the fuel needed to heat one large tub of water. The heat goes from fuel to water to human body and does not have to warm the air in all the rooms of the house as it does in most American and European homes today. Of course, a Japanese bath will not, by itself, keep someone warm where winters are very cold. Then additional heating is needed.

Today the hot bath is an old, well-loved tradition in Japan even in homes where more modern methods of heating make it unnecessary solely from the point of view of keeping warm. It can, however, lower the temperature at which a person finds a room comfortable.

Fireplaces and Furnaces

Since long before the beginning of history, human beings have used fire to keep warm in cold weather. The earliest fires were built out in the open—like campfires—and probably were used for both warmth and cooking. Because air is such a poor conductor of heat, heat leaves the fire largely in two ways: by convection and radiation.

As the fire warms the air about it, this warmer air rises in a convection current that usually can be easily seen because smoke rises with it. Heat rises with it, too, and this heat is lost. The fire also radiates heat in all directions. A person is warmed by the heat that radiates in his direction, but only on

Two methods of transfer of heat from a fire.
Heated air rises in a convection current (left), and
heat radiates in all directions from the fire (right).

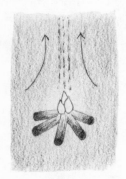 

the side facing the fire. This is why, as you sit before a campfire, your face and hands may be uncomfortably hot while your back is cold, for your
back receives no radiation. A campfire may keep a
person from freezing to death, but it is not totally
comfortable.

Sitting before a fire in the house can be somewhat more comfortable, for there you are protected
from rain and snow and strong winds. However, if
the house is not to become filled with smoke, there
must be at least two openings—one through which
the smoke rising in the convection current can escape from the house and another through which
the air that replaces it can enter. In very simple
homes, like grass huts, igloos, or other one-room
dwellings, there can be a hole in the roof for escape
of smoke, and any other opening—door, window,
or even cracks or chinks in the walls—can serve as
the place of entry. In other words, there must be a
draft in the house, and the draft carries heat away
and brings in cold air. As with a campfire, a person
is warmed primarily by radiation.

If the house is made of straw, wood, or other
inflammable materials, care must be taken to prevent its catching fire. The fire can be laid on a
hard-packed dirt floor, which will not burn. In this
case the house cannot have a second floor, or if it
does, not a heated one. If there is a second floor,
care has to be taken that the convection current

In a medieval, one-room house some heat was lost in a convection current that rose to the hole in the roof directly over the fire laid on the dirt floor. Heat radiating from the fire warmed the room, but this was not very efficient.

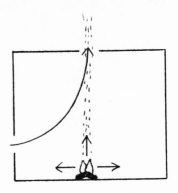

from the fire is directed away from it to prevent its filling with smoke. In ancient and medieval times houses were often only one story high, especially in places where the winters were cold. In some parts of Europe houses were simply one large room. Everyone—family members, visitors, and servants—lived in the same room and gathered around its central fire for warmth.

About a thousand years ago the weather in Europe was milder than it is now, and people probably survived the winters in homes warmed by only a single fire in the floor without a great deal of discomfort. Then, about the thirteenth century (the 1200s) the weather began to cool slowly but gradually; this continued for several centuries until the weather was so cold that this period became known as the Little Ice Age. A large drafty room with a single fire in the middle of the floor did not provide much comfort then.

As the weather began to cool there came a great advance in heating a house safely: the fireplace and chimney, which were lined with stone or bricks. The stone or bricks made the fireplace and chimney fireproof, and relatively large fires could be built safely inside the house. Furthermore, rooms on the second or third floor could have their own fireplaces, for each chimney conducted the

A fireplace and chimney lined with bricks (shaded). Heat was still lost in convection currents (left), but because the back of the fireplace reflected radiated heat (right), the fireplace was more efficient than a fire laid on a bare floor. If the fire is laid on a grate, a convection current rises through the fire itself and causes more efficient burning.

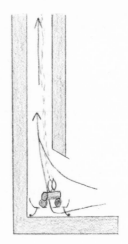 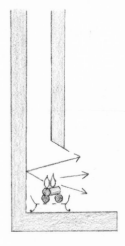

convection current of smoky air from its own fire
directly out of the house. In addition, heat radiated
from the fire to the back wall of the fireplace was
reflected back out of the front of the fireplace.
Therefore less wood or coal had to be burned to
warm the people gathered before the fire. Bricks
are better reflectors of heat than are stones, and so
they are used more often in fireplaces than stone.

If the wood or coal was placed on a metal
grate rather than directly on the floor of the fireplace, part of the convection current rose through
the fire; this brought more oxygen directly to the fire
and made the fuel burn more nearly completely.

There were still disadvantages to fireplaces,
however. There had to be a draft, and a great deal
of heat produced by the fire was lost through the
chimney. In very cold weather, when people sat
before the fire, their faces were still too hot, and
their backs too cold. In cold winters the only warm
places in the house were immediately before the
fireplaces or near the kitchen stove.

The old-fashioned kitchen stoves made of cast
iron and containing a wood fire were, of course,
meant primarily for cooking and baking, but some
of the heat of the fire was conducted across the
metal walls of the stove and from there radiated
into the kitchen. Smaller versions of the big kitchen
stoves were metal wood-burning stoves that are still
popular today for auxiliary heat or even for heat-

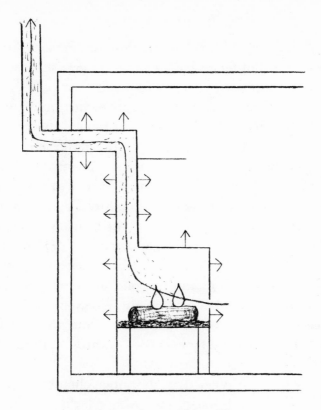

A metal stove is something like a fireplace brought into the room. While heat is still lost through the convection current that rises in the stovepipe, heat radiates to the room from the metal sides and top of the stove and the metal stovepipe.

ing entire small houses. The stovepipe that carries smoke and convection currents out of the house itself serves as an additional radiator, which conserves some of the heat that would otherwise escape up the chimney.

Another great improvement in heating came with the furnace, which is the primary source of heat in most modern homes. Once again there was a single fire in the house, but now it warmed all the rooms; this method of heating is called central heating. In early versions of the furnace, heat was produced by burning coal, and the heat was moved about the house by a convection current. Although there was some variation in these furnaces, they all consisted to two chambers, one inside the other. The inner chamber, called the *firebox* (or *firepot*), was connected to the chimney. From the outer chamber a series of ducts led upwards to each of the rooms of the house.

Coal was burned in the inner chamber, and the smoke and some heat escaped through the chimney. As the fire warmed the metal wall of the firebox, heat moved by conduction across the wall and into the air of the outer chamber. From there it rose by convection currents through the ducts and into the upper rooms. As the air warmed the rooms, it cooled and sank down in other ducts that returned it to the furnace where it was rewarmed and recycled.

There was a grate in the bottom of the firebox through which cinders (small chunks of unburned

coal) fell into a small box at the bottom of the furnace. From here the cinders could be shoveled out.
The cinder box usually had a small opening to
bring air to the firebox through the grate. This

An early style of coal furnace. See text for
details.

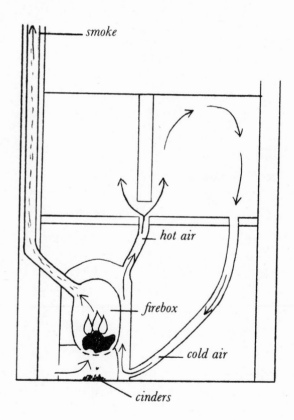

smoke

hot air

firebox

cold air

cinders

opening either was connected directly to the out-doors by means of its own duct, or it simply opened into the basement. In the latter case, a window somewhere in the house—usually a basement win-dow—was kept partially open. The incoming cold air replaced the air lost through the chimney and brought oxygen to the fire.

A big advantage of such a furnace over a fire-place is that, because heat moves within the rooms by convection currents, each room is heated nearly uniformly, and the people are warmed by the air around them—not by a fire on only one side of a room. In addition, although the fire itself still needed a draft, that draft went directly from the furnace to the chimney and not through the rooms.

Most modern homes are heated by variations on the early coal-burning furnaces. Other fuels, such as oil or natural gas, may be used to heat the air, and the furnace may have a fan to hasten the movement of the warm air. In some furnaces water rather than air is heated and circulates to the rooms. In these cases the water is heated in a boiler connected by pipes to radiators in the rooms to be warmed. Hot water or steam rises by convection (or hot water is pumped) to the radiators. Heat ra-diates from the radiators and warms the room. This cools the water or steam (which condenses to water) which moves downward in other pipes that return to the boiler.

In all these types of central heating, something—air or water—is heated, circulates to the rooms of the house, loses some of its heat there, and returns to the furnace where it is reheated. Such a system provided more nearly uniform heat than does a fireplace.

Solar Energy

Today, as in the past, a fire heats most homes, but a few houses are warmed by solar energy—light from the sun. In only a few places in the world— where the winters are not severe and where most winter days are sunny—can solar energy provide all the heat that a family needs. Solar energy can be used, however, to supply part of the heat needed. In some cases it is used only to supply hot water for bathing, dishwashing, and laundry.

One thing needed for solar heating is a substance that absorbs light and converts it to heat. This substance, once warm, must be protected from losing the heat to the environment. This is usually done by enclosing the light-absorbing substance in a space surrounded at least in part by glass. The glass allows light to enter but prevents wind from blowing warm air away.

If you have ever been in a greenhouse, which is composed almost entirely of glass, you know how hot it can be there. Even on a very cold winter day,

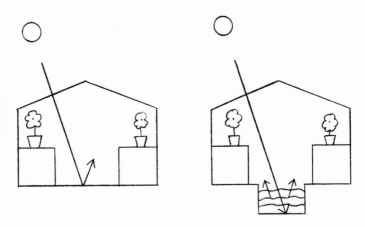

(left) A greenhouse is heated by day by sunlight that enters through the glass roof and walls, is absorbed by some substance, and radiates back as heat. (right) If the absorbing substance is something that stores heat—such as water—the heat is radiated back slowly and can keep the greenhouse warm for a longer period of time.

as long as the sun shines brightly, it can be hot in a greenhouse with all the doors and windows closed. Visible light passes through the glass windows and strikes objects in the greenhouse. Some of the light may be reflected back out through the glass, but some of it is absorbed and converted to heat. Because heat escapes relatively slowly through the glass, during hours of bright sunlight, heat accumulates in the greenhouse.

At night, when no sunlight shines on the glass windows, but when heat escapes slowly but continuously, the greenhouse cools. If the nights are cold and long, the greenhouse will be cold long before morning. If, however, there is something in the greenhouse that can store heat and release it slowly, the greenhouse will not cool so fast during the night. Because water can absorb a great deal of heat without becoming very warm itself and because water releases this heat very slowly, a large pool of water in a greenhouse can keep the greenhouse a little cooler by day and a little warmer by night. Of course, this alone is not enough to prevent the greenhouse from becoming very cold partway through the long winter night.

Heating homes by solar energy depends basically on the same kinds of events. Light shines on a light-absorbing substance enclosed in some transparent material (usually glass). Either this substance stores the accumulating heat or it may transfer it to another substance.

Some homes with greenhouses on their south wall may use them as a source of auxiliary heating by a method very like that described for the greenhouse alone, except that in this case convection currents carry warm air from the greenhouse into the upper rooms of the house, and the cooled air returns and is rewarmed by the heat being released by the water. Of course, if this is not enough to heat a greenhouse alone in cold weather, it is not enough to heat the house, either. In the coldest parts of winter they both need central heating.

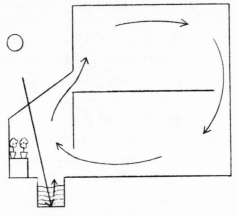

A greenhouse attached to a house can be used as an auxiliary source of heat. There must be two openings—an upper and a lower—through which convection currents can move from the greenhouse into the house and back again.

In another method of heating a house by solar energy, the south wall is almost entirely glass. A few feet inside the glass wall are racks containing large drums of water. The south faces of the drums are painted black. The black paint absorbs the light that shines on it and converts it into heat, which is conducted to the water in the drums. In sunshine, the drums accumulate heat faster than they radiate it. At night, they continue to release heat and warm the house. This type of solar heating may be sufficient to keep people comfortable

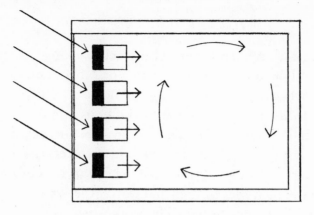

*In this type of solar energy heating,
sunlight enters through a glass wall
and strikes the black-painted ends of
drums of water, which store the heat
and radiate it slowly into the room.
Convection currents distribute warm
air in the room and return it to the
drums.*

for nearly the entire winter in mild climates. Only if there is a run of many cloudy days would there be need for additional heat from a furnace or fireplace.

In another method of solar heating, solar energy collectors on roofs absorb light and convert it to heat that is stored elsewhere in the house, usually the basement. One type of roof solar energy collector uses copper tubing, folded back and forth many times, to give it a great deal of surface area. The tubing is enclosed in a case with a black backing and a glass cover. The black backing absorbs sunlight and heats the water (or other fluid) that moves through the tubing. The tubing connects with a pipe that runs into the house and then to some storage area. The hot water, for example, might run into a large tank and then return to the solar collector on the roof where it is reheated. With each recycling of the water, the water in the tank becomes hotter. The tank, then, is a storage tank for the accumulated heat, but it is also more.

This tank is a countercurrent heat exchanger. Within it is another copper pipe bent or coiled

(a) A house with solar energy collectors on the roof. (b) A portion of a collector seen in section; sunlight strikes a black absorbing substance which becomes hot and loses heat to water circulating in copper pipes. (c) One section of a solar energy collector; as the water passes along the pipe it becomes hotter (dark shading). (d) A combination storage tank and countercurrent heat exchanger. (e) An air duct that is another countercurrent heat exchanger that warms air that will heat the rooms. Note that the water circulating in the coiled pipes moves in the opposite (counter) direction to that of the water that warms it (d) and the air it warms (e). Not shown in this drawing are the pumps that keep the water moving, the fan that moves the air, and the insulation that keeps this equipment from losing heat.

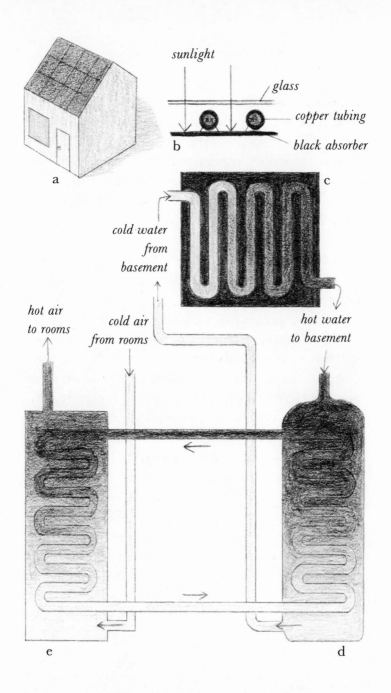

sunlight

glass

copper tubing

black absorber

b

a

c

cold water
from
basement

hot air
to rooms

cold air
from rooms

hot water
to basement

e   d

many times to provide a great deal of surface area through which the water in this pipe can absorb heat from water in the tank. If this house is heated by hot air, then this pipe with its hot water runs into a second countercurrent heat exchanger, but in this case cold air returning from the rooms of the house flows over the hot pipe and removes heat from it. The heated air rises, warms the rooms, and returns cooled. The hot water, which has been cooled by the cold air, returns to the first countercurrent heat exchanger (the storage tank) and is rewarmed.

There are many variations in the way solar energy is trapped and stored for use. However, we still have not devised economical and efficient ways either to capture enough solar energy or to store enough heat to warm homes over long cloudy periods during very cold winters. Much research is being done now to solve these problems.

Because solar heating does not always provide sufficient heat to keep a house as warm as we would like it, it is very important that not only the pipes and tanks holding hot water be well insulated so that they lose as little heat as possible, but that the entire house should be insulated as well. Conscientious homeowners fill the spaces within the outer walls of their houses with insulating material and lay it on attic floors. But even with these precautions, the truth is that most of our dwellings

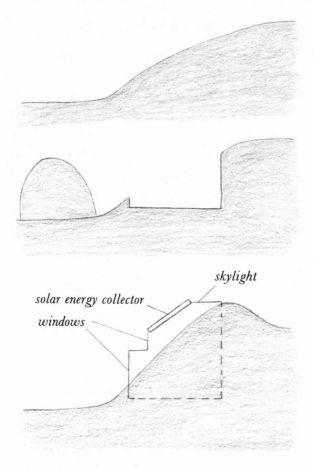

solar energy collector

skylight

windows

A few new houses today use earth as insulation.

stick up out of the ground and into the air, where they are subject to the cooling effect of all the winds that come their way.

Today a small number of new homes are being built partially underground. The earth dug up for the basement is saved, and when the house is completed, the earth is piled around the north, west, and east sides of the house. Large windows are located on the south side of the house and so are the solar energy collectors if the house is to have them; there may also be skylights in the roof. If the property has sloping ground, the builder may take advantage of this by building the house into the slope. It is interesting that these new homes rely partially on a very old type of insulator, the ground itself, and the house has become a partial cave, one of the oldest types of home used by human beings.

Appendix

Here are some helpful hints about keeping warm and keeping cool.

Keeping Warm

1. Wear thick clothing that will retain body heat and prevent wind from reaching body surfaces. Wool, fur, and some synthetic fibers* are best.

---

* Theoretically, any kind of fiber can keep you warm if it is arranged so as to enclose many tiny air spaces. Cotton batting used as insulation in a jacket can keep you just as warm as an equivalent quantity of wool as long as the cotton batting remains fluffy. But cotton (and linen, too) becomes packed down quickly, and this destroys the air spaces. Wool fibers, on the other hand, have a crimp to them that keeps them springy, so wool does not pack down easily. Therefore, wool (and the furs with hairs that stay in their more or less upright position) retain their air spaces and are "warm" materials. Whether synthetic fibers are "warm" or "cool" depends not so much on the actual substances from which they are made but on whether the fibers do or do not pack down, and this depends on how the fibers were manufactured.

2. Several layers of moderately thick cloth-ing—flannel shirts, sweaters, long underwear—are usually warmer than one very thick layer of cloth-ing. Layers also allow you to take off one or two garments if you begin to feel too warm. This is especially important if you are working hard out-doors in winter and do not want to perspire under your clothing, for as the clothing becomes damp it loses its insulating qualities.

3. Wear clothing with long sleeves and long pants or skirts. Sleeves should have tight cuffs. Fit long pants into boots outdoors. Garments should button up tight at the neck (they can be unbut-toned if you become too warm). A turtleneck sweater is good.

4. Keep your ears and hands covered with a hat (or earmuffs) and mittens or gloves when out-doors. Mittens are better than gloves, for they do not let cold air come between your fingers. In very cold weather wear mittens over a pair of gloves. A scarf can be worn around the neck, and a loose end used to protect your face from the wind. If it is very cold and windy, wear the scarf around your face, leaving only your eyes free for seeing your way.

5. Wear dark clothing by day. It will absorb sunlight and convert it to heat.

6. Wear your hair long—at least long enough to cover your ears.

7. Keep your skin dry. This is especially im-

portant for your feet, so winter boots should be waterproof as well as warm.

8. If you have to remain outdoors in cold weather for a long time, try to keep moving. Your body produces more heat when you are active than when you are still. If you have to stand in one place for a long time, wiggle your fingers and toes several times, let them relax for a moment, and then repeat as long as necessary. This should improve the circulation in them and help to keep them warm. Keep your legs together and your arms against your chest so as to present the least amount of surface area to the wind.

9. If, because of a sudden change in weather, you have to walk some distance in bitter cold weather without adequate clothing, remember that paper is a good insulator. If you can get a newspaper, take four or five sheets and tear a hole big enough to accommodate your head in the center. Take off your outer garment, slip the newspaper over your head so that one side of the paper covers your chest and the other your back. Replace your outer garment. Tear a few layers of newspaper so as to make some "inner soles" and "uppers" to put inside your shoes. If you have mittens, line them with paper, too. If not, line your pockets with paper and keep your hands in them. If you have a hat or scarf, try to use them to hold some newspaper around your head.

10. If you are ever truly lost in the woods during a blizzard and cannot see any clues as to which way to proceed, the best thing to do is to take whatever shelter you can. First look for a spot sheltered from the wind—a clump of bushes, a stand of evergreen trees, or anything else that will break the wind. In the best place you can find, dig a small hole in the snow for yourself, to get more shelter from the wind. Line the bottom of the hole with branches or brush—evergreen branches are best—so that there will be insulating air spaces between you and the snow when you sit or lie down. If you can line the sides and top of the hole with more branches, so much the better. You may not be comfortable, but you will have a better chance of surviving than if you walk around aimlessly, exposing yourself to cold winds.

11. To keep your house warm, keep the doors and windows closed. Doors should have weather stripping, and any chinks or cracks should be repaired. However, the house should not be a sealed box. A little fresh air should be allowed to enter the house to avoid indoor air pollution.

12. Open curtains and draperies and raise shades in windows on which the sun is shining. At night, and on north windows during the day, lower shades and close all curtains and draperies.

13. A hot bath or shower early in the evening will heat your body. Several layers of clothes (flan-

nel pajamas and a woolly robe, for example) will help to retain your body heat. Water evaporating from the bath will raise the humidity of the air in the house and will make it seem warmer than it is.

Keeping Cool

1. Wear thin, light-weight clothing that will transmit perspiration and allow it to evaporate. Cotton, linen, and some synthetic fibers (see footnote on page 189) are best.

2. Wear as little as possible, especially in humid weather. Wear loose, sleeveless clothing open at the throat. One exception: if you have to work in bright sunshine, a light layer of clothing over all your body will protect you from the sun.

3. Wear light-colored clothing, preferably white, by day. It will reflect light away from you before it can be converted into heat.

4. If you wear a hat, wear one with a broad brim that will shade you. If the hat has holes in it—as in a loosely woven straw hat—heat will not become trapped within the hat or under the brim.

5. Wear sandals or other shoes with openwork.

6. Wear your hair short; keep your ears exposed.

7. Try to be less active physically than usual; stay in the shade as much as possible.

8. Be sure to drink enough water to replace

what you lose in perspiration; your thirst will tell you how much you need.

9. A few minutes in a swimming pool will take a lot of heat from your body, so will a few minutes in the bathtub or shower—use the coolest water that is comfortable for you. You can get a similar effect, but not so long-lasting a one, by soaking a terrycloth washcloth in cold water, wringing it just until it is no longer dripping, then placing it on some bare skin. As the water evaporates, it will cool your body. If the air is very humid, you may have to direct the breeze of a fan on the cloth to increase the rate of evaporation. When the cloth dries, wet it again.

10. To keep the house cool, close curtains and draperies and lower shades in windows on which the sun is shining.

11. For the first or second day of a heat wave you can often keep the house comfortably cool by closing all doors and windows by day to keep hot air out and opening them at night when the outdoor temperature is cooler than the temperature in the house. They should be closed again early the next morning *before* the outdoor temperature rises.

12. Closing doors and windows also slows the entrance of humid air into the house. If the weather is humid, keep doors and windows closed at night as well as by day. This method will usually work for only the first day or two of a heat wave.

13. When the indoors become too warm to be comfortable, a breeze may help. Because convection currents move from cool to hot places, from low to high places, and from small to large openings, open partially a basement window on the north (which is probably the coolest) side of the house and open wide a window on the first (or second) floor or in the attic on some other side of the house. This should set up a convection current that brings the cooler air from the basement to the living area of the house and that carries warm air out of the house. An attic fan or window fan facing outdoors will hasten the process.

14. If you live in an apartment, open the lower halves of windows on the north (or shady) side and the upper halves of other windows.

15. If you are trying to cool just one room with only a single window in it, open the window a small way from the bottom, and more from the top. Air should enter from below and leave from the top.

16. Avoid cooking as much as possible.

17. If you take a hot bath or shower, keep the bathroom door closed and the window open to allow the humid bathroom air to escape from the house.

Suggested Readings

ADAMS, ROBERT W. *Adding Solar Heat to Your Home.* Blue Ridge Summit, Pa.: Tab Books Inc., 1979.

BAHADORI, MEHDI N. "Passive Cooling Systems in Iranian Architecture," *Scientific American* 238(2): 144–154 (February 1978).

BAKER, MARY ANN. "A Brain-cooling System in Mammals," *Scientific American* 240(5): 130–139 (May 1979).

BENZINGER, T. H. "The Human Thermostat," *Scientific American* 204(1): 134–147 (January 1961).

BOURGEOIS, JEAN-LOUIS. "Welcoming the Wind," *Natural History* 89(11): 70–75 (November 1980).

CAREY, FRANCIS G. "Fishes with Warm Bodies," *Scientific American* 228(2): 36–44 (February 1973).

COON, CARLETON S. "Man Against the Cold," *Natural History* 70(1): 56–69 (January 1961).

DOUGLAS, MATTHEW M. "Hot Butterflies," *Natural History* 88(9): 56–65 (November 1979).

EDHOLM, OTTO G. *Man—Hot and Cold.* London: Edward Arnold, 1978.

FEUERLICHT, ROBERTA STRAUSS. "The Cones of Cappadocia," *Natural History* 82(4): 50–57 (April 1973).

FRITH, H. J. "Incubator Birds," *Scientific American* 201(2): 52–58 (August 1959).

HEINRICH, BERND. "The Regulation of Temperature in the Honeybee Swarm," *Scientific American* 244(6): 146–160 (June 1981).

HELLER, H. CRAIG, LARRY I. CRAWSHAW, AND HAROLD T. HAMMEL. "The Thermostat of Vertebrate Animals," *Scientific American* 239(2): 102–113 (August 1978).

HILEY, PETER. "How the Elephant Keeps Its Cool," *Natural History* 84(10): 34–41 (December 1975).

IRVING, LAURENCE. "Adaptations to Cold," *Scientific American* 214(1): 94–101 (January 1966).

LE MAHO, YVON. "The Emperor Penguin: A Strategy to Live and Breed in the Cold," *American Scientist* 65: 680–693 (November-December 1977).

LÜDSCHER, MARTIN. "Air-conditioned Termite Nests," *Scientific American* 205(1): 138–145 (July 1961).

MORSE, ROGER A. "Environmental Control in the Beehive," *Scientific American* 226(4): 92–98 (April 1972).

Natural History 90(10) (October 1981). The entire issue is devoted to ways of keeping warm.

RONALD, K., AND J. L. DOUGAN. "The Ice Lover: Biology of the Harp Seal (*Phoca groenlandica*), *Science* 215: 928–933 (February 19, 1982).

SCHMIDT-NIELSEN, KNUT. *Desert Animals: Physiological Problems of Heat and Water.* New York: Oxford University Press, 1964.

————. "Countercurrent Systems in Animals," *Scientific American* 244(5): 118–128 (May 1981).

STONEHOUSE, BERNARD. *Animals of the Antarctic: The Ecology of the Far South.* New York: Holt, Rinehart & Winston, 1972.

TWITCHELL, MARY. *Wood Energy: A practical Guide to Heating with Wood.* Charlotte, Vt.: Garden Way Publishing, 1978.

WELSCH, ROGER. "Shelters on the Plains," *Natural History* 86(5): 48–53 (May 1977).

WITTOW, G. CAUSEY. "Sun, Sand, and Sea Lions," *Natural History* 83(7): 56–63 (August-September 1974).

WIK, OLE. *Wood Stoves: How to Make and Use Them.* Anchorage, Alaska: Alaska Northwest Publishing Company, 1977.

Glossary

ARTERY: one of the blood vessels that carry blood toward the heart

ARTERIOVENOUS ANASTOMOSIS (AVA): a type of fine blood vessel found especially in animals adapted to survival in very cold climates; AVAs connect arteries and veins directly; when arteriovenous anastomoses are dilated they release a great deal of heat to the tissues in which they are located and keep them from freezing

ATOMS: the smallest particles of which the elements of the universe are composed

AVA: arteriovenous anastomosis

BARB: one of the branches of the shaft of a feather

BARBULE: a projection from the barb of a feather

BLUBBER: a thick layer of fat under the skin of whales, seals, penguins and some other marine animals; blubber insulates these animals from the cold water or serves as a food supply or both

BROOD PATCH: a bare spot on the breast or abdomen of some birds incubating eggs or young chicks; the brood patch forms by the dropping of feathers and by an increase in the number of capillaries in the skin

Glossary

CAPILLARIES: the finest of the blood vessels in the body; in most cases they receive blood from the arteries, release food, oxygen, and heat to the tissues, pick up waste products, and return blood to the veins

CAVERNOUS SINUS: in dogs and some other panting animals, a structure in which cooled blood from the nasal chambers cools blood flowing in arteries to the brain (see page 114)

CELSIUS SCALE: a temperature scale devised by Anders Celsius, a Swedish astronomer; on the Celsius scale the freezing point of water is $0°$, and its boiling point is $100°$; to find the Celsius equivalent of a temperature given in Fahrenheit subtract 32 from the Fahrenheit temperature and then divide the answer by 1.8:

$$°C = \frac{°F - 32}{1.8}$$

CENTIGRADE SCALE: the former name for the Celsius temperature scale

COLD: the lack of heat; the sensation of a lack of heat

"COLD-BLOODED": a term popularly applied to poikilothermic or ectothermic animals

CONDUCTION: one of three ways that heat is transferred; in conduction heat is transferred by the motion of molecules (or atoms)

CONVECTION: one of three ways that heat is transferred; convection depends on the rising of a warm gas (such as air) or liquid (such as water)

Glossary

CORE TEMPERATURE: the temperature of the innermost parts of the body; ordinarily this is the normal body temperature of an animal

COUNTERCURRENT HEAT EXCHANGER: a device in which heat passes from a warmer current to an adjacent current flowing in the opposite direction

ECTOTHERM: an animal that is warmed mostly by external heat

ENDOTHERM: an animal that is warmed primarily by the metabolic reactions occurring within its body

FAHRENHEIT SCALE: a temperature scale devised by Gabriel D. Fahrenheit, a German physicist; on the Fahrenheit scale the freezing point of water is 32° and its boiling point is 212°; to find the Fahrenheit equivalent of a temperature given in Celsius, multiply the Celsius temperature by 1.8 and then add 32 to the answer:

$$°F = (°C \times 1.8) + 32$$

FIREBOX: the inner chamber of a furnace that holds the burning fuel

FIREPOT: see firebox

FLIPPER: a broad, flat forelimb (as of seals, whales, and penguins)

GRATE: a metal framework in a fireplace, furnace, or stove on which burning wood or coal is placed; cinders and ashes fall through the grate, and air rises through it

HEAT: a form of energy that causes the temperature of bodies absorbing it to rise

Glossary

HOMEOTHERM: an animal whose temperature ordinarily remains virtually constant (within a very small range of temperature—a degree or two) despite great environmental temperature variations

HONEY: a thick, syrupy solution of sugar in water made by bees that collect nectar and evaporate much of the water from it

HYPOTHALAMUS: a part of the brain that has among its several functions the maintaining of normal body temperature

IGLOO: an Eskimo house made of snow blocks

INCUBATE: to warm eggs by sitting on them or curling around them

INFRARED RADIATION: a form of invisible radiation by which heat is transferred across a vacuum or through the earth's atmosphere

INSULATION: any substance or combination of substances that conducts heat slowly

METABOLISM: all the chemical processes occurring in a living thing; most metabolic processes release heat

MOLECULAR MOTION: the movement of molecules, by which heat may be conducted

MOLECULE: the smallest combination of atoms of which a chemical compound is composed

NECTAR: a usually thin, watery solution containing sugar and produced by flowers; bees make honey from nectar by evaporating much of the water from it

NEURON: a nerve cell; neurons transmit nervous impulses ("messages") from one part of the body to another

PANTING: a deep, rapid breathing that cools the blood of dogs, cats and certain other animals

PARKA: a fur pullover garment with a hood; a parka usually extends down to the hips or knees

PERSPIRATION: a watery secretion (containing a low concentration of dissolved salts and other subtances from the body) that is forced by blood pressure from the blood into sweat glands and from there onto the surface of the skin; evaporation of perspiration cools the blood

PILO-ERECTOR MUSCLE: a small muscle associated with the base of a hair; when a pilo-erector muscle contracts, it causes the hair to stand more nearly erect

POIKILOTHERM: an animal whose body temperature ordinarily varies with the environmental temperature

RADIATION: one of three ways that heat is transferred; when transferred as radiation, heat travels with a wave motion

RADIATOR: something that radiates heat (or other types of radiation, such as light)

SET POINT: the temperature at which a thermostat is set; also the normal body temperature of an animal (if the set point is raised, as in some diseases, fever results)

SHAFT: the main axis of a feather

SOD: the upper few inches of grassland soil containing the living roots of plants; also, a piece cut from such soil

SWEAT GLANDS: glands in the skin of a few animals (especially human beings) that secrete perspiration

TEMPERATURE GRADIENT: a change in temperature over a distance

THERMOSTAT: a device that regulates temperature in a building by turning on or off the furnace or air conditioner; in the human body and in the bodies of some other animals, a part of the hypothalamus acts as a thermostat and regulates body temperature

THORAX: the middle of the three main sections of the bodies of bees and other insects; the wings are attached to the thorax, which contains the flight muscles

TUFF: a soft volcanic rock formed from lava and ash

VEIN: one of the blood vessels that carry blood away from the heart

"WARM-BLOODED": a term popularly applied to homeothermic or endothermic animals

WATER VAPOR: water in a gaseous form in the air; water that has evaporated

Index

Alacalufe Indians, resistance
  to cold, 113
Arabs, Bedouin
  clothing, 132–136
  tents, 143–145
arteriovenous anastomosis
  (AVA), 109–112
AVA
  See: arteriovenous anasto-
    mosis

bees
  See: bumblebees *and* hon-
    eybees
behavior, 56–95
  burrowing, 57–61
  huddling, 67–70
  orienting to sun, 61–64
  surface area, increasing
    and reducing amount of
    exposure, 64–70
  water, cooling with, 70–75
  young, care of, 76–95
birds
  care of young, 78–86
  feathers, as insulation,
    50–53

blubber, as insulation, 52–55
body temperature, 3–11
brood patches, 78
bumblebees, shivering, 8

camels
  homeothermic and poiki-
    lothermic characteris-
    tics, 7
  huddling, 68–70
  humps, 55
  orienting to sun, 61
  size, 36
  sweating, 99
  woolly coat, 50
capillaries, 79
  and AVAs, 109, 110
  and countercurrent heat
    exchangers, 106, 107,
    114–116
  and sweat glands, 97
caribou, hollow hairs, 48
cavernous sinus, 114, 115
caves, 145–148
clothing, 125–140
  of Arabs, 132–136
  of Eskimos, 136–140

Index